BLOOD
WILL
OUT

ALSO BY WALTER KIRN

BLOOD WILL OUT

THE TRUE STORY *of* A MURDER,
A MYSTERY, *and* A MASQUERADE

WALTER KIRN

LIVERIGHT PUBLISHING CORPORATION

A Division of W.W. Norton & Company

New York • London

For information about permission to reproduce selections from this book,
write to Permissions, Liveright Publishing Corporation, a division of
W. W. Norton & Company, Inc., 500 Fifth Avenue, New York, NY 10110

For information about special discounts for bulk purchases, please contact
W. W. Norton Special Sales at specialsales@wwnorton.com or 800-233-4830

Manufacturing by Courier Westford
Production manager: Anna Oler

Library of Congress Cataloging-in-Publication Data

Kirn, Walter, 1962–
Blood will out : the true story of a murder, a mystery,
and a masquerade / Walter Kirn. — First edition.
    pages cm
ISBN 978-0-87140-451-0 (hardcover)
1. Gerhartsreiter, Christian, 1961– 2. Kirn, Walter, 1962–
3. Impostors and imposture—United States—Case studies.
4. Murderers—United States—Case studies. I. Title.
HV6760.G47K57 2014
364.152'3092—dc23

                                                2013046327

Liveright Publishing Corporation
500 Fifth Avenue, New York, N.Y. 10110
www.wwnorton.com

W. W. Norton & Company Ltd.
Castle House, 75/76 Wells Street, London W1T 3QT

1 2 3 4 5 6 7 8 9 0

For Amanda Fortini, my love, and in memory of my mother, Millie Kirn

He was versatile, and the world was wide!

—PATRICIA HIGHSMITH, *The Talented Mr. Ripley*

A writer not writing is practically a maniac within himself.

—F. SCOTT FITZGERALD

BLOOD
WILL
OUT

ONE

I T FELT LIKE a noble gesture at the time, and I was in the mood for an adventure. The summer my wife was pregnant with our first child and President Clinton was slipping toward impeachment, I volunteered to drive a crippled dog from my home in Montana, where it was being cared for by patrons of our local Humane Society, to the New York City apartment of a rich young man, a Rockefeller, who had adopted it on the Internet.

His first name was Clark. We met over the phone. I called him as a favor to my wife, Maggie, the Humane Society's president, who was trying to help out Harry and Mary Piper, the people who had rescued the poor creature after she was run over by a car. They'd paid for the surgery that saved her life, arranged for her to be treated with Reiki massage, and taught her to use a canine wheelchair whose tires did the work of her paralyzed hind legs. The heirs to a Minnesota banking fortune and devout Episcopalians (Mary was in training to become a priest), the Pipers had recently taken Maggie and me to dinner and complained about the difficulty of transporting the dog to the East Coast. They feared entrusting her to a commercial airline because of her perilous condition, and though Clark had told them that he owned a plane, he said it was tied up in China with his wife, Sandra, an international management consultant. When I heard about this, I offered to play the middleman, in part as a way of assuaging my guilty conscience over the death of one of Maggie's shelter dogs I'd hit with my pickup truck a few months earlier. But I had another reason altogether for wanting to speak with Clark: I was a writer, even more importantly, a writer between books, and I had a hunch I was going to meet a character.

Clark opened our initial call with the story of the adoption. He told me he'd learned of the dog, whose name was Shelby, through a Web site devoted to finding owners for homeless Gordon setters, a breed that he prized for its links to British royalty and for its bounding, avid temperament. He knew instantly that he wanted her, he said, and had been trading e-mails with the Pipers in his quest to convince them that he should have her. His building was only a block from Central Park, meaning that Shelby would have ample room to exercise and "engage in morning squirrel hunts." What's more, Clark volunteered, in the apartment under his lived Manhattan's "top veterinary acupuncturist." He said he'd already spoken with this healer and felt confident that, with his help, Shelby would someday make a full recovery.

"I'm afraid that's unlikely," I said. "Her spine was crushed. I'm not sure you know this, but there's a possibility that somebody shot her before she was run over."

"Have you ever been treated with acupuncture?"

"Well, no," I stammered.

"Then you remain unacquainted with its magic."

The call lasted over an hour, derailing my day. I was on deadline that morning for *Time* magazine, working in my small office above a western-clothing store to convert a stack of raw reporting produced by various stringers around the country into an intelligible story about some matter of popular sociology—TV violence, children of divorce—that couldn't be dealt with in a hundred pages but that I had to summarize in four. I didn't particularly like the job but I was in dire need of money just then, having recently borrowed half a million dollars to buy a five-hundred-acre ranch ten miles north of the town of Livingston in what a poetic realtor had described as "the shadows of the Crazy Mountains." The place was a picturesque ruin of sagging fences, overgrazed pastures, and broken-down corrals whose hayfields were irrigated by shallow ditches riddled with rattlesnake dens and badger holes. The house had a kitchen with a toilet in it, out in the open, not far from the sink, and its top floor was abandoned and boarded shut. I'd bought the place to fulfill a dream of self-sufficient country living, but I was discovering that paying for it would mean working harder than I ever had at assignments much drearier than I could bear. The scariest part was that my loan—a private contract with the ranch's old owner, a podiatrist from Billings—stipulated that I could lose the place if I missed even a single monthly payment.

Clark did most of the talking during the call. He told me a lot about himself, and much of what he told me was hard to process without the ability to see his face and know if he was joking or exaggerating. He told me he'd never gone to high school. He told me he collected modern art but that he found it ugly: "Pure puke on canvas." He told me he only ate bread he baked himself. He told me he owned another Gordon setter named Yates on whom he lavished three-course meals prepared from fresh ingredients by his private chef. He asked for the number of my fax machine so he could send me copies of the recipes.

"You actually write these recipes out?" I asked him.

"My people do," he said.

While I waited for the document, drinking cold coffee at my cluttered desk and ignoring the beeping of my phone line (my editors at *Time* were trying to reach me), I asked Clark what he did for work. My hunch was that he did nothing at all.

"At present," he said, "I'm a freelance central banker."

I asked him to explain.

"Think of a country's money supply," he said, "as a lake or a river behind a dam. Think of me as the keeper of that dam. I decide how much water flows over its turbines at what velocity, and for what duration. The trick is to let through sufficient water to nourish and sustain a country's crops but not so much that it floods the fields and drowns them."

"Which countries," I asked Clark, "do you do this for?"

"At the moment? Thailand."

"That's a lot of responsibility."

"It's fun."

"Which countries before Thailand?"

"That's confidential."

"This can't be a common profession."

"We invented it. My company did, I mean. Asterisk LLC."

He spoke with an accent, clipped and international, and occasionally tossed in a word, like "erstwhile" or "improprietous," that seemed to tie a bow on the sentence that included it. I judged his peculiar manner to be the product of a profoundly insulated upbringing. I recalled meeting a few people like him in college at Princeton—pedigreed, boastful, overschooled eccentrics who spoke like cousins of Katharine Hepburn—but I'd been raised in rural Minnesota, deep in manure-scented dairy country, and I'd never succeeded in getting close to them. Their clubs wouldn't have me, I didn't play their sports, and I found them a bit repulsive physically, what with their prematurely thinning hair and delicate, intestinal-pink skin. After college, while studying at Oxford on a fellowship, I'd managed to mix with some of their British counterparts, even Princess Diana's younger brother, but I was just a novelty to them, a vulgar New World entertainment. When my time at Oxford ended, I hung on in London for several months doing clerical work at a small law firm and tearing around with a crew of titled party boys. In truth, I couldn't keep up with them. The cabs. The bar tabs. Eventually I flew back to America and landed a job at *Vanity Fair* writing punning headlines for fluffy stories about Nancy Reagan's Italian gown designer and Sting's wife's charity activities, but my boss didn't like that I stayed in at night instead of throwing myself into the social scene and I was fired within a year.

But Clark seemed to like me, and to want me to like him. When the dog menu started creeping from the fax machine, it persuaded me of his eagerness.

> *2 cups freshly cooked brown rice*
> *1 green vegetable (usually green squash) finely ground in*
> *food processor*
> *1 yellow vegetable (usually carrots) finely ground in food*
> *processor*
> *1 clove garlic finely ground in food processor*
> *1–2 lbs. raw fatty beef, ground fresh in food processor*
> *just before feeding*
> *or 1–2 lbs. cooked ground turkey/chicken*
> *or 1 can salmon*
> *some kelp powder, 1 TBS brewer's yeast, some bone-*
> *meal, 2 TBS wheat germ, some bee pollen*

Reading over this mad, painstaking document, I resolved to meet Clark in the flesh, should I ever get the chance. As a novelist, I'd be guilty of professional malpractice if I didn't try.

He still wasn't finished trying to impress me. As though he thought it would burnish his credentials for the role of the setter's adoptive parent, he told me that he lived next door to Tony Bennett, whom he said he could hear rehearsing through the walls at night. He told me that he had degrees from Harvard and Yale, where he'd studied economics and mathematics. He told me that he could sing the words to any song that I might name to the tune of the theme from *Gilligan's Island*, and he demonstrated with a Cole Porter lyric. He told me that he'd learned from "sources" that Prince Charles and the Queen had murdered Diana with the help of a team of crack commandos, and he said that he knew from speaking with a close friend (the Admiral of the Navy's Seventh Fleet) that the People's Republic of China and the United States had recently signed a secret treaty allowing the Communists to invade Taiwan, without opposition, at their convenience.

"That's the story of the coming century: Chinese *Lebensraum*," he said. "We're back in the 1930s before the war, and it's not going to end well. Prepare yourself, Walter. I warn you."

"How?" I said.

"Precisely."

"I'm serious. How?" I asked. "Because, frankly, I'm with you on some of this."

"On China?"

"On the general drift toward global conflict."

"Here," Clark said, "is how it soon shall be. Japan will be the front porch of their new empire, whose might will push out to Australia and New Zealand. We will retreat to Hawaii, a shrunken power, and a new hemispheric order will take hold. In time, we'll be forced to renounce our Western alliances as we submit to the interests of the East. Indeed, this is what's happening already; it simply has yet to be publicly announced."

When I mentioned to Clark that I reviewed books for *New York* magazine, he told me that just a couple of days earlier he'd written a book review himself—his first ever, for Amazon.com. He directed me to it while we were on the phone and insisted that I read it then and there on my computer. The book in question was *Conversations with God: An Uncommon Dialogue* and the review was titled "Move Over, L. Ron Hubbard, Here Comes Neale Donald Walsch." Its lofty, scolding, condescending tone was poorly matched to its sophomoric prose:

Neale Donald Walsch, a writer with a clear God-complex, presumes to speak for God in an imaginary conversation of mostly upper-case "Me" sentences . . . Written in Question and Answer format and almost all short words and sentences that even Hemingway could not have made any shorter, the book should have appeal to the marginally literate. Its Do-Whatever-Feels-Right philosophy should give anyone enough justification to live a 1960s Free Love lifestyle. In my favorite line, p. 61, God said through Mr. Walsch that "Hitler Went to Heaven."

"Book sounds bad," I said when I was done.

"But what do you think of the review?"

There are certain subjects that I can't lie about, so I tried to be diplomatic. "Well, it's spirited."

Finally, we got down to business about the dog. Clark lamented the fact that his plane was indisposed, and he let it be known that he didn't drive. He asked me if Shelby might be sent by train. I told him the train would take days and wasn't dependable—if Amtrak even carried animals. Then I brought up the idea of hiring a courier. I offered to find one, negotiate a price, and handle all the necessary arrangements.

"I'm afraid that won't do," Clark said.

I asked why not.

He answered with a long litany of his bad experiences with "service people," from greedy plumbers to dishonest maids. They faked injuries. They filed lawsuits. They pilfered family heirlooms. It was such a shame. Society had changed. People had lost all sense of personal honor—people at every level, low and high. Indeed, it was the people at the top, in government but particularly in business, whose lack of integrity most discouraged him.

"I'd rather not use a stranger for this job. I'd rather entrust it to a friend," Clark said. "To be candid, I have security concerns."

Out my window, half a mile away, a coal train was grind-
ing and clanking its way through town, and my mind suddenly wandered. I led a strange existence in Montana, the
result of many strange decisions. Eight years earlier, in the
spring of 1990, I'd come here from New York to report on
a religious cult that was preparing for Armageddon. The
leader of the cult, a middle-aged woman who claimed to
channel the spirits of such fabled figures as the Buddha, Sir
Francis Bacon, and Merlin, was urging her followers to leave
their homes and move to a bomb shelter dug into a moun-
tainside. I bought one of these houses for a low price (the
End of the World creates motivated sellers), thinking I'd use
it as a writing retreat. I ended up staying. Five years later,
impulse struck again. After a ten-month courtship, I married Maggie, the nineteen-year-old daughter of the novelist
Thomas McGuane and the actress Margot Kidder. I was
thirty-four. I did things my way. Now, three years later, we
had a baby coming and lived on a ranch that I'd purchased
on a whim and had no notion of how to run.

"Are we out of ideas?" Clark said.

He knew we weren't. As I'd told the Pipers at dinner the
previous night, I'd done the drive to New York City before.
Three years earlier, a few months after our wedding, I'd
signed a short lease on a small loft located in Manhattan's
Flower District, feeling cramped in a town of seven thousand
scandalized by my marriage to a teenager. I'd also needed a
break from my new mother-in-law, who had moved back to
Livingston to be near Maggie after having lived here in the

1970s during the town's chaotic bohemian heyday. Margot's brief marriage to Maggie's father had been an outlandish cultural period piece, torrid with stimulants and infidelity, and her return to the scene unbalanced her. A few months after my wedding, she broke down on a visit to Los Angeles, ran through the airport fleeing imagined killers, flung away her dentures and her purse, and turned up days later in suburban Glendale living under a hedge in someone's yard with almost all her hair chopped off. She returned to Montana to rest and gather her wits. The next thing I knew she was sitting in our living room being interviewed by Barbara Walters, whose crew and equipment forced me from the house and onto our front steps, where the neighbors had gathered, seeking Barbara's autograph.

I couldn't skip town soon enough. I packed up my car, put Maggie on a plane, and hurled myself into a wet gray prairie blizzard that didn't let up until I reached Saint Paul, where I decided to proceed through Canada rather than via Chicago and the southern route. I finally calmed down as I approached New York. Why hadn't I just stayed in Manhattan, I wondered now. Because I couldn't afford to, I remembered. The city had cleaned itself up during my absence and real estate prices had arrowed off the graph. The crack epidemic that was raging when I left had been replaced by a luxury condo epidemic. Worse, my old Princeton friends were getting rich, in some cases thanks to having bought such condos just as I was skedaddling to Montana. Their clothes came from shops that I felt unworthy to enter and their wedding receptions featured bands that made real records, records that reached the charts.

Before Clark and I were off the phone, I'd made up my mind to drive the dog myself. It took another call to make arrangements, but by the time he proposed a "handsome stipend" as a token of his "boundless gratitude," we both understood the terms of our new friendship. He would delight me with comic songs and dog menus and access to a circle I'd thought closed to me, and I would repay him with the indulgent loyalty that writers reserve for their favorite characters, the ones, it's said, we can't make up.

TWO

I F I'D MET the dog first, I might never have met Clark. I might have refused to take the trip. Her fur was black with spots of rusty red, and her frail, wasted body was tapered like a mermaid's. On the day I went to pick her up, she lay on the floor in the Pipers' living room and gazed at us through moist, beseeching eyes fringed by lashes flecked with dust and dandruff. I could see every rib, every knob along her spine. The feeling she roused in me wasn't pity or sadness, but a sort of primitive revulsion. My instinct was to back away from her, to distance myself from her scourged, drained, shriveled spirit.

Instead, I crouched down and petted her bony skull. She took no apparent pleasure in my touch, just huddled and trembled, aggressively pathetic, while the Pipers beamed approval on her.

"We're going to miss our Shelbatron," Harry said, apparently referring to her dependency on the prosthetic K-9 Kart. His wife slid a comforting arm around his waist. "It helps to know she's found the perfect home."

The Pipers believed that Shelby's survival was the work of God himself, helped by the prayers of the people at their church. They were dog people, a type I'd never be. Dog people hail from an old branch of humanity that remembers in its chromosomes what it is like to hunt and sleep with animals. Dogs, to them, are beings sent down from heaven to test our capacity for love. The article about Shelby that Mary had written for the Gordon Setter Club of America (the article that attracted Clark, presumably) concluded with these lines: "I am a big fan of rescue—as the Scriptures say (and bear with me those who are not religious)—'Do not forget to entertain strangers, for by doing so, some people have entertained angels without knowing it.'"

Harry was as kindhearted as his wife, perhaps because of a trauma from his childhood. His father had been a partner in a large brokerage firm, Piper, Jaffrey and Hopwood, that was based in my home state of Minnesota, and his mother, Virginia, a famous Twin Cities society figure, had been the victim of the highest-ransom unsolved kidnapping in American history. I met Harry when he'd asked for my opinion of a book he was writing about the crime, which happened in 1972, not long before the Patty Hearst abduction, which pushed it from the headlines. After paying one million dollars for his wife's freedom, Harry's father was directed by the perpetrators to a secret spot in the northern Minnesota woods where he and Harry, who was in his teens then, found Virginia lashed to a tree trunk. The coiffed and gowned socialite Harry knew from home had been replaced by a shivering wild beast caked in its own feces. He felt revulsion, and then shame for feeling it. Seeing his mother in her disheveled state had colored his view of her afterward, he told me, and he hoped that the book might somehow purge his troubled conscience.

Before I could leave on what I'd estimated would be a three-day drive to the East Coast (Maggie planned to fly out and join me when I arrrived, both to meet Clark, who intrigued her, and to enjoy a weekend city holiday before her November due date drew too near), I had to learn to put Shelby in her wheelchair. I tenderly slipped my arms beneath her and carried her outside to the yard. Through her skin I could feel the outlines of her organs—spongy, faintly rounded objects that seemed to be floating loose inside her body. The source of her feeble life force was hard to locate. Her heart didn't beat; it just very lightly tapped, like a grasshopper jumping inside a paper bag.

The wheelchair was a spidery contraption fabricated from some lightweight metal and equipped with several straps and slings that held Shelby's paralyzed back end in place,

preventing her legs from scraping on the ground or rub-
bing against the tires. Because her legs were more like ropes
than limbs, getting them into the harness was a challenge.
Finally, I tied on her booties, two leather pouches meant to
shield her back feet in case they dragged.

We repeated the procedure so I'd remember it and could
teach it to Clark.

"Time for our girl to show off," said Harry. "*Come!*"

Shelby jerked forward in her metal armature. The first
stretch of progress was easily achieved; it took only a tiny
pulse of will to turn the axle and the two spoked wheels.
Then the wheelchair sped up and reached a downhill
grade, panicking Shelby with its momentum. She twisted
sideways as though to get away from it, staggered, yelped
in reflex, and turned around as if to bite the thing. Harry
went to calm her. This took awhile. After her panting
slowed and she stopped trembling, he walked away and
ordered her to come again.

I felt sick. The whole exercise seemed doomed. Harry had
said that Shelby was improving, that she'd come a long way,
a miraculously long way, but the quavering manner in which
she held herself convinced me that she'd started to slip again.
In my pocket was the first cell phone I'd ever owned, bought
to update the Pipers and Clark during the trip. Should I use it
to call him in New York and cancel our arrangement? He'd
want a good reason. He might even get angry; he had a certain peevish streak, I'd noticed. Most rich people did. They
wanted what they wanted when they wanted it.

Harry and I freed Shelby from her prosthesis and lifted her into the cab of my Ford pickup truck. His help was symbolic, like a pallbearer's—I could have done the job myself—and it complicated the maneuver, nearly causing us to drop her. Once she was situated on the seat and had resumed her natural shapelessness, Harry stepped back and finally let the tears crash. Mary looked down. His crying was hard to watch, startlingly primal and disfiguring, with sources beyond those in the present, it seemed.

"Please drive safely," he said.

"I will. I always do."

"You have your phone?"

"It's right here in my pants."

"She's Clark's now," he said. "She's little Shelby Rockefeller."

Harry produced a glass vial from his shirt that contained water from the Sea of Galilee. He flicked a few drops at Shelby on the seat and sprinkled a few more on the truck's hood. The night we'd had dinner I'd told him about the shelter dog, a hyperactive, big-boned mutt named Miles, that had leapt in front of the truck that spring while I was driving into a hayfield. Miles's head appeared above the hood line, his tongue lolling horribly from his open mouth, and then he vanished, followed by an articulated crunch that I felt through the steering wheel in both my wrists. I braked and backed up, then jumped down out of the cab and gathered the broken black body in my arms. The trip into town with Miles across my lap, jerking and slackening, leaking life and spirit, prepared me for nightmares that, strangely, never came. I braced myself for them; they never came. Their absence was a subtle form of punishment, denying me the catharsis that I craved.

After the ritual of the holy water, Harry asked us to join hands and close our eyes. His prayer, which was fervent, petitioned the saints and angels to watch over me and Shelby as we traveled and guide us safely to our destination. He also asked the spirits to smile on Clark, to bless him with wisdom, fill his heart with love, and grant him the gift of healing as Shelby's keeper.

When we opened our eyes again, I was free to go.

I WASN'T IN ANY shape for a long drive. I'd worn myself out that spring and early summer driving 120 miles each way back and forth between Livingston and Billings, Montana's largest city, where I was reporting a cover story for *Time* on methamphetamine abuse. The photographer with me had covered foreign wars but said that he found Billings after dark scarier than Zimbabwe or Beirut. I insisted on full immersion in the dark atmosphere and made us stay in a cowboy-themed motel with brown cartographic stains on its thin mattresses. We followed the addicts around from bar to bar, lighting and relighting their bent cigarettes and listening to their fierce paranoid raps about UFO microphones sewn into their scalps and underground cities of scheming Jewish bankers. The photographer owned a police band radio that we kept turned on inside my car so we could race to drug-related crime scenes. We happened on stabbings whose victims were still bleeding and chain-swinging riots in pit-bull trailer courts. In my glove compartment was a loaded pistol—a macho secret that bred a rugged attitude—and in my jeans was a bottle of Ritalin, a drug that I sometimes used when writing on deadline. When the pills hit my bloodstream I felt brisk and competent, a hard-boiled reporter in an old movie, but once they wore off I grew touchy and distracted. The only antidote was another pill, dissolved in a can of soda for faster action. I built up quite a tolerance this way, for both Ritalin and Dr Pepper.

Between my nights on assignment I played rancher, wrestling with the tools of western agriculture—shovels, post-hole diggers, and wire stretchers. I liked the ranch; having grown up in the country, I'd never done well in towns and cities. Urban landscapes made of language, bristling with cautions, promotions, and announcements, kept me thinking, even in my sleep. In the old days, I'd used liquor to smooth things out. But on a trip to New York in 1992 I had my last drink, a double shot of vodka on top of two sleeping tablets I'd taken earlier but decided were duds when they didn't work immediately, allowing me to rush down to a bar located close enough to my hotel that I judged I could make it back to bed in case they did start to hit. I timed things terribly. I woke in an alley behind a Chinese restaurant with grains of fried rice on me that I thought were maggots. I'd learned my lesson, but only about booze. Pharmaceuticals still had much to teach me.

Maggie was feeling poorly from her pregnancy. She rejected more food that spring than she consumed and seemed frustrated by the progress of the remodeling job that I was doing myself with two paid helpers, one of whom was a listless aging junkie who drilled through walls into current-bearing wires and clogged the toilet almost every time he used it. We'd passed through the stage when you talk about the baby—what its room will be like, whose features it will have—and into the one where you watch the TV news and wonder, without saying anything out loud, why you ever decided to reproduce. Or maybe only I wondered; aside from her nausea, Maggie seemed happy enough. My fear of fatherhood wasn't normal fear, though; instead of releasing adrenaline, it sapped it, producing a stony, inert fatigue, as though I'd been injected with heavy plastic. Sometimes, if I had an article to write, I took Ritalin in my office or at home, followed by Ambien to bring on sleep. The Ambien only worked for a few hours, and I would wake in a dream state and raid the kitchen, preparing weird mashes of flour and pancake syrup that I would find smeared on dishes in the morning. Sometimes I also found e-mails to old girlfriends and misspelled, unpunctuated notes for lurid short stories with outlandish settings, including, once, a brothel in the Arctic.

My last trip to Billings had been especially harrowing. I met up with a source, a twenty-year-old addict who'd abandoned her toddler during a three-week meth spree, and drove with her to an abandoned house where she was squatting with three male friends who were living off welfare checks that she was still receiving even though her child was in foster care. I interviewed them in the kitchen. It was empty except for a pyramid of beer cans assembled with such maniacal precision that no light could be seen between the cans; they stood four feet high where the table should have been. The tweakers were cooperative at first but things disintegrated when they asked the girl for her check and she answered that she'd lost it. (She'd told me it was hidden in her underwear.) One of her friends dumped her purse out on the floor while another went upstairs and came back down with an army-style rifle. He pointed it at me and my photographer and asked who we really worked for. "*Time*," I said. But who owned *Time*? I tried to tell him. The girl started trying to talk him down, allowing me to slip out with the photographer. We drove a circuitous route to our motel, but the Ritalin in me convinced me we'd been followed. Too jumpy to sleep, I cracked the blinds and monitored the parking lot all night.

AT THE END OF the Pipers' driveway I stopped my truck. Beside me, on a plywood platform that I'd made myself and covered with a green blanket, Shelby lay with her nose stuck in a vent. In front of us was the immense Montana sky. White clouds were stacked up to the atmosphere's curved ceiling and monumental disclosures seemed at hand. I lit a cigarette to prepare for them and entered a frontage road that served I-90, exhaling sideways through my rolled-down window. At some point I looked down and to my right and saw Shelby's nostrils, the most responsive part of her, gaping wide as though to pull the smoke in. I blew a small puff at her, experimenting, and saw that her tobacco hunger was real. A legacy of the master who'd abandoned her? Or was it some campfire reflex from ancient hunting times, when man and dog and spear and pipe were one?

Someone called my new phone a few miles into the drive, but when I picked up I couldn't hear a voice—the signal was too weak. In case it was Clark, I tried his number, but I was confident he wouldn't answer; all phone calls had to originate with him. It was a privacy measure, one of many. He'd also told me he used his Rockefeller name only with friends and family, never in public. The phone rang and rang when I called it; no machine. He'd said he didn't like answering machines because the tapes or computer chips inside them could fall into untrustworthy hands.

Within an hour of setting out, I'd learned all there was to know about the challenges of driving a dog without a functioning nervous system in the back half of its body. The main problem was that Shelby couldn't brace herself; she was helpless against centrifugal force. When I hit the brakes or rounded a curve, she'd pinball around inside the cab, slamming against the dashboard and the door. I fastened her in with a seatbelt but she hated it and protested by chewing at the buckle. Afraid that she'd break her teeth, I set her free and positioned her with her head across my lap and my right arm pressing firmly on her neck. This steadied her but it distracted me, forcing me to bear down at critical moments when I should have been focused on my driving.

About twice an hour she had to pee. She didn't whimper or fidget when the urge came, but we were becoming psychic, the two of us, intimately dual, and I knew in my muscles when she had to go. I'd start scanning for places to pull over, but it was Montana, where freeway exits are rare, so I would find myself weighing up the cost of letting her wet herself inside the truck versus the risk of parking on the shoulder, unprotected against hurtling semis. The first two times this happened, I chose safety, but once the green blanket was reeking of ammonia I decided to stop no matter what.

My end of the deal, where peeing was involved, meant lifting her down from the truck onto the ground and holding her under the belly while the urine drizzled from her urethra. It drizzled because the nerve damage she'd suffered prevented her from directing it. Once, at a rest stop, the urine soaked my arm, creating the problem of how to dry my arm. I could walk to the bathrooms and fetch a paper towel, but since I couldn't leave Shelby lying there helpless, I either had to carry her in with me or lock her in the truck. The truck was closer. Once I got her into it, my dripping arm had wiped off on her fur. The problem had solved itself, though not in a way I felt good about.

I didn't much care by then. I was in despair.

The air conditioner gave out near Billings and filled the cab with the toxic smell of engine coolant. A short distance on, I ran over a length of steel-belted tire—what truckers call a "gator"—that seemed to put my alignment out of whack. I regrouped and refueled at a truck stop with a casino that attracted the desperate meth types familiar to me from my reporting. I kept an eye on them loitering near the building— for some reason they always came in couples, often a pasty, heavy, braless woman with a wolfish, jiggly-eyed man—as I set down the red plastic bowl I'd brought along and filled it from a jug of water. But without her chair to hold her upright so she could get her head over the bowl, Shelby couldn't lap the water. I unfolded the chair and worked to get her into it. I had to push her face in the bowl to make her drink, but she refused to unfurl her pink tongue, which wasn't as pink as a dog's tongue ought to be. It was gray, gray like freezer-burned meat. I grabbed her chin and pushed a thumb and finger in between her jaws to wedge them open, then poured the bowl of water over her snout. A little went down, but she choked and coughed it out. I was crying by then, and in the purest way—the way people cry when there's no one around who cares and they can stop or carry on as they please. And so they carry on; they might as well.

"Shelby, you have to drink for me," I said.

I was starting to wonder what might befall a person who disappointed a Rockefeller.

I QUIT DRIVING THAT night in Forsyth, Montana, having gone only a couple hundred miles. Forsyth was a town of dumpy storefronts that would have gone out of business in healthier places where people still expected to make money, but here there was no reason to abandon them, since the owners weren't selling things from them anymore, just using them as ringside seats to watch the bar fights, furtive pain-pill swaps, weeping fits, and stray animal attacks of final-stage social collapse on the great plains.

At a convenience store I bought a Gatorade and strapped Shelby into her wheechair for a walk. This drew glances, and one looker approached me, a man with bowed legs and a deeply concave chest that looked like it had been crushed under a boulder. He was smoking a little cherry-scented cigar that stayed in his mouth when he asked me, "What's the deal there?," touching one foot to the edge of Shelby's chair. "This worth it?" he said. I wasn't sure what he meant. Was it worth it for the dog or me? "Barely," I said. I expected a wry laugh. Instead, the guy pressed me on my destination, knowing it couldn't be Forsyth. "New York," I said. "It's kind of a story."

"Well, I hope so, this poor thing."

"A Rockefeller adopted it," I said. I was curious how this would play in the real world, and this was that, a place as real as dirt.

"Good people," he said. "Broad thinkers. I've met a few."

"Where?" Montana can surprise you. The towns may be hurting, but out on the big ranches live many fugitive millionaires, titans even.

'I used to coach track at prep schools in the East. I knew

their kids. They raise them tight and trim. No brats. No." He kneeled down and petted Shelby's head, then cleared some gunk from her eye with a long fingernail. "This doesn't seem like a city dog to me, though. Twitchy. Not settled."

"I'm only doing a job."

"That ignorant thing people say, they rule the world? Not true. Not anymore at least. The Rockefellers are mostly broke now. No one runs the world, I'm sad to say. They don't even try. It was better when they did."

The motel I chose was an old place beside some railroad tracks that charged a cleaning fee to guests with dogs. I didn't tell the clerk I had a dog. This was a habit I'd picked up from my father: saving nickels and dimes through petty lies. He was a patent lawyer in Saint Paul who planned to retire to Montana to fish and hunt. I didn't look forward to having him nearby. Since his divorce from my mother eight years ago, our lifelong clash of temperaments had sharpened. I found him aggressive and overbearing. He found me self-deluding and neurotic. My therapist urged me to cut him off completely but I continued to call him on holidays and when I had important news. He knew about the ranch and Maggie's pregnancy, but not much else about my recent life. He didn't know a thing about my trip. This was too bad; I suspected he might approve. Action delighted him. Boldness was his creed. "Hit the other guy harder than he hits you," he'd taught me in my schoolboy football days, but it was plainly all-around advice. I'd heard he was scary in courtrooms and often won settlements simply by scrambling the other lawyers' nerves. He drank black coffee straight from a Thermos and his cars were littered with shot-gun shells and jackknives that he used to cuts swatches of fur from roadkilled deers to use in tying trout flies.

My mother was different. She believed in caution. I planned to stay over at her house when I reached Minnesota the next evening. She lived in the same little green Tom Sawyer river town where I'd grown up and gone to school, a retired ER nurse who liked to read the classics, play the piano, pay calls on housebound neighbors, listen to conservative talk radio, and write in her journal about her son's accomplishments. It had been almost a year since I'd last seen her, which was a long stretch for us. I missed her when we were apart, but sometimes when we were together she unnerved me. Her stoicism. Her reserve. I couldn't tell when she was angry at me, which allowed me to think she rarely was, but now and then I caught a twinge, a flicker.

This happened when I told her about Clark. My description of his quirks amused her, reminding her of Bertie Wooster from her beloved P. G. Wodehouse novels, but she grew quiet when I mentioned the trip, and even quieter when I brought up Shelby. She wasn't an animal person to begin with—she had asthma and allergies, and fur was filthy—but what seemed to bother her in this case were the expenditures the dog had caused. How much had the wheelchair cost? The surgeries? Did I want to put all those miles on my truck? She didn't ask these questions outright but they were implied in her silences and pauses. I also thought I detected a harsher charge, aimed at me alone, of genuflection.

In the motel in Forsyth, Shelby dreamed and whimpered on the floor. I lay in bed and listened to the trains making their heavy-breathing diesel noises and their shuddering, gigantic coupling sounds. I skimmed a book I'd tracked down a couple of days ago: Steinbeck's *Travels with Charley*, the true account of a cross-country road trip taken in a pickup with a poodle. The book was published in 1962, the year that I was born, and I thought it could serve as a model, or a foil, for the book that might be forming inside me. Preserving a sense of literary purpose was crucial to my self-respect tonight. It might also prove crucial tomorrow with my mother, who would want a higher reason for my exertions than the servicing of a rich eccentric.

The Steinbeck book was not what I expected. My impression was that it consisted of folksy sketches of charming American characters and scenes, but it was gloomier than that. In a section set in Minnesota, Steinbeck drives an evacuation route intended to help people survive a nuclear war. He calls it "a road designed by fear." He crosses the Canadian border and then reenters the United States, grumbling about the stern, impersonal guards and how modern governments diminish people. He frets that TV is flattening the culture and voices disgust at materialism and wastefulness. Pretty much the only state that pleases him, because it seems clean and honest and unspoiled, is Montana, the place that I'd just left.

The book depressed me. It brimmed with fears about the future that had mostly come true. I put it down. My phone was turned off, because those were still the days when turning a phone off wasn't considered hiding. My silence would have to assure Clark I was coming. When I finally showed up with Shelby, if we made it—if the sounds she was making in her sleep weren't symptoms of a failing nervous system—he'd witness a marvel that no one ever tires of: faith in a stranger rewarded in full measure. He trusted me, who trusted very few, and he was right to trust me, for here I was, heading his way through the hot Montana badlands where dinosaur fossils lay scattered across dry creek beds and pale, ribbed fingers of eroded stone offered moody perches to hawks and vultures. Still, I felt a rising qualm—not about Clark, about myself. Would it be wrong to write about him someday? If I masked his identity? If I changed his name? He knew I was a writer—we'd discussed it; he'd even done some "scribbling" himself. But did he know what a writer really *is*?

Probably not. Few people do. A writer is someone who tells you one thing so someday he can tell his readers another thing: what he was thinking but declined to say, or what he would have thought had he been wiser. A writer turns his life into material, and if you're in his life, he uses yours, too.

SHELBY SOILED MY MOTHER'S kitchen rug the moment I helped her roll into the house. My mother's place was a tribute to English cottages of the sort that Miss Marple might visit to solve a murder, all bookshelves and lamps and lace antimacassars, with so many welcoming nooks to sit and read in, so many helpful side tables and ottomans, that the question of how to best get comfortable there was a bit overwhelming—just too much choice. On me, the house's effect was soporific, and happily so; the sleep I usually got there was soft, upholstered, deep, enveloping. It was the sleep of a prized and cared-for son, impossible to achieve in other settings. To benefit from this maternal service, though, required appreciative tidiness from me—no drinks without coasters, all throw pillows replaced—and Shelby's disgusting act when we arrived ruined the atmosphere, setting it on edge.

"Out. That dog goes out," my mother said.

She had me settle Shelby on the porch, under a bird feeder hectic with wrens and chickadees. I folded her wheelchair and leaned it against a wall. "It's ugly, that thing. It upsets me," my mother said. She was a small woman with olive skin and complexion-contrasting blue eyes whose power was their ability to narrow decisively yet minutely, also instantly, leaving a person to wonder what had shifted—my mother's facial expression or the weather. Once she passed judgment on something, the issue was closed. There could be fighting about it but no winning.

When I came back inside after fussing with the chair she made me wash my hands with Ivory soap and gave me a fresh towel to dry them on. The towel went straight into the washing machine along with the clothes that I had on. My other clothes were in the truck, but I was forbidden to bring my bag inside. My mother gave me a robe and made me shower and waited for me in her leather reading chair, beside the stand where she displayed her dictionary and kept her curated kit of reading tools: her fringed leather bookmarks, her colored pencils, her ivory-handled magnifying glass.

"I'm going to say this," she said when I sat down.

"I can't. I'm sorry, Mom. It's not my dog."

"I want you to put it down," she said.

"I know why you might think that but I just can't."

"This is absurd. It doesn't have a life. It can't even scratch itself, for heaven's sake. Who is this man, anyway?"

"Clark?"

"There's something wrong with him. Anyone who'd want that animal, there's something wrong with him, I'm telling you. Which branch of the Rockefellers is he from?"

"That's not the kind of thing we talk about."

"How old is he?"

"My age. I don't know exactly."

"Who's his grandfather? Nelson? David? Laurance?" My mother was a consumer of big biogaphies and knew her major lineages cold. Tudors, Plantagenets, Kennedys, Shrivers. The woman belonged on genealogical *Jeopardy!*

"Mom, I'm not up on that stuff," I said. "I need to sleep."

"I'm going to say something else to you."

"Okay."

I knew what was coming: nothing. She'd go quiet. She'd let me imagine something. A trick of hers. She'd look at me, I'd look at her, and then I would make some excuse to look away. I hated it. I'd hated it since child-hood. Maybe the new way to play things would be to say so.

"I hate this, Mom," I said. "I hate this one."

She let the silence chill and thicken. In the window behind her the air was turning green, the color it gets in rural Minnesota when pelting hailstones are building inside black clouds and farmers are herding their animals indoors. Our small town was a strict, efficient moral universe where even the elements collaborated to help make the points that needed to be made.

"I need to bring her back inside," I said.

"I'll only allow it if you put her down."

"This is out of my hands," I said. "I made a promise."

"Phooey, Walt," my mother said.

I COULDN'T RESUME THE trip. With a nurse's discernment, my mother saw my pallor, the trembly way I cut and ate my pancakes, my too-tight grip on my glass of grapefruit juice, and wouldn't permit me to get back on the road. She gave the order at the breakfast table, and for once I was happy to yield to common sense. I'd slept for ten hours, hard. I'd left the earth. When I woke up, I couldn't move my body. My legs felt strapped to the mattress, my bowels were stone. Some deep, blocked channel had opened in my skull and freed a sludge of stagnant mucus that shifted and cracked behind my eyes and temples. The paralysis felt retributive and just and I lay there in bed for a while not fighting it, letting Shelby's predicament be mine.

This sacrificial exercise succeeded: when I finally dragged myself downstairs, Shelby was drinking water and looked revived. My mother had laid a green garden hose in front of her, turned it on at minimal pressure, and she was lapping at the stream with a quickly curling, uncurling tongue.

Over breakfast my mother and I devised a plan. I called Northwest Airlines and booked a flight that left that night, a nonstop to LaGuardia. I had to pay full fare: four hundred dollars. I said I'd be taking a dog, but not what kind of dog. The agent reminded me that I'd need papers proving that she'd had her vaccinations. I didn't possess such documents, but my mother knew how to get them: across the street from her lived a kindly bachelor veterinarian. We called his office, drove there, got the shots, obtained the papers, and paid his fee, which he freely admitted was twice his normal fee. "Emergency service," he said. I didn't buy it. My mother had told him the story and dropped Clark's name—she couldn't help herself. What the vet should have said was, "Rockefeller service."

He also wrote out a prescription for tranquilizers—my mother's idea and the key to the whole scheme. Stuff Shelby into a pet crate, knock her out, pack her wheelchair in a plain brown carton, lug it all up to the ticket counter, smile. The only snag was Clark: he had no answering machine. Unless he was home in the middle of a weekday to pick up his phone, he wouldn't know to meet us.

But he was there. It was fine. He wasn't at work. Come to think of it, all of our other conversations had also occurred during weekdays. He'd called me, though—called me from his office, I assumed. And yes, I remembered him saying he had an office. But maybe he didn't go there much. Maybe he made his own hours. Or he was sick today.

"I apologize for the surprise, the change of schedule. But my truck's running funny," I said. "And Shelby's tired." I glanced at my mother across the kitchen table; she'd come over to my side, as she always did, though sometimes her principles slowed her down at first. "Actually, we're both tired. It's been a rough one."

"I love surprises. I'm thrilled. Great news," Clark said. He didn't sound sick at all. He sounded tip-top. What mattered to me, however, was that he sounded grateful.

At the airport, drugged and crated, Shelby passed into the airline's baggage system. A freight handler carried her through an unmarked door and she was no longer my responsibility. I boarded the plane and fell asleep immediately, progressing through some filmy mental membrane into a realm of private imagery. I'd like to say I remember what I dreamed of, but all I truly remember was that I did; the trip had brought on a psychedelic fever. I woke as the plane was passing over New Jersey, that brawny industrial landscape of tanks and docks, freight yards and pipelines, America's loading area, and then we were crossing the lighted Manhattan skyline, as furrowed and labyrinthine as fate itself. I remembered the first time I saw it. I was ten. My parents had decided that my brother and I should see the great national landmarks of the East: the Liberty Bell, the Capitol, Boston Harbor, the USS *Constitution*. We drove. We stayed with people—friends and distant relatives—who'd made the mistake at some point in the past of idly inviting us to visit. The trip was punishing. New York came last. I'd grown jaded by then: the monuments we'd toured had all turned out to be smaller than I'd hoped or hedged in by unmagnificent surroundings. Not this one. As we approached the Lincoln Tunnel, I beheld a stupendous all-in-one new universe that instantly diminished the one I'd known. Here was the centerpiece, all else was backdrop. The place looked ancient, but in a modern way, and it had an ark-like self-assurance, as though it expected to ride out vast catastrophes that would devastate those who weren't its passengers.

The plane met the runway with a squealing noise and all the alarming, thrilling bumps and shudders. Underneath me in the cargo hold Shelby was waking up, I hoped; I'd timed the administration of the tranquilizers so that Clark might meet a conscious animal, one capable of responding in some fond way when its new owner at last laid hands on it. The trip had been hard, and I wanted it to end well, in a way that was worthy of my stipend. I'd performed, in the old sense, the classic sense, a labor, the kind imposed on people by fickle gods. For once it had not been an intellectual labor but physical, emotional, and real. And I'd endured. I'd persisted. I'd come through.

THREE

H E SAID I would recognize him by his resemblance to the actor David Hyde Pierce who played the character of Niles, the brother, on the TV comedy series *Frasier*. It was one of my mother's favorite programs, so I knew Niles well. He was slim, fey, balding, and he wore suits. The first time my mother made me watch the show with her, my impression was that Niles was gay because the script portrayed him as an opera buff, but later in the program he mentioned a girlfriend. Because I'd been called gay at Princeton for writing poetry, and at Oxford for writing plays, I abhorred any stirrings of bigotry in myself, but when Clark compared himself to Niles, his tone of voice conspicuously pleased, I'd wondered if he were testing me sexually as other gay men whom I'd known had when I met them. But Niles wasn't gay, of course, he only seemed to be, and only to rubes like me, so probably not. What Clark was testing in me, if anything, were my feelings about prim and prissy upper-class types. I liked them just fine, was the answer. They had their place.

I looked around for Niles's and Pierce's double as I stepped off a crowded escalator into LaGuardia's baggage claim area. Was that him? Too stout. Was that him there? Nah, too grim. I didn't like this guessing game; I didn't think it should have to be a game. He could have told me how he'd be dressed, as I'd done. Blue denim button-down shirt, black jeans, and sneakers. I didn't care to impress him, this outfit meant. I was from Montana, my own man.

"There are you are, Walter! Welcome to New York."

Clark, who seemed shorter than the TV actor and lacked his swan-like bearing, was wearing a pink billed cap and a pink polo shirt. His hair, what little I could see of it, was a tampered-with, unconvincing shade of blond. His glasses had thick, dark plastic frames and looked like they ought to come with a fake mustache attached. He had on khaki trousers and no socks. Beside him was a nervous-seeming woman who stood a step back and blurred into the background. It was Sandra, his wife. He briefly introduced us and then ignored her as he inquired, with an ornate, ambassadorial air, about my flight. I'm not sure how I answered him. All flights that land safely are much the same to me.

The luggage carousel creaked into motion and bags started sliding down out of a chute and battering one another at the bottom. A few minutes later all of them were gone and there was still no Shelby. Concern for her distracted me from Clark, who was buzzing on about something I hadn't caught. I found him instantly annoying; a twee, diminutive hobbit of a fellow whose level of self-amusement seemed almost delusional. In his speech, as I'd noticed during our phone calls, he observed the outward forms of wit, as though speaking humorously came down to algebra (*it's not the X of Y that bothers me, it's the Y of X*) and how one filled in the variables didn't matter. If he thought this way, he was working the wrong audience. I only laugh at truly funny remarks; it's the one incorruptible, honest trait in me. Maybe he was nervous, though. His fake hair color spoke of a baseline insecurity, as did the cap, which I suspected concealed a bald spot.

While he prattled, an airline worker emerged from somewhere bearing the unwieldy plastic pet crate. It looked blessedly undamaged. Clark knelt down and peered through its front grate, making dog-lover sounds—little clucks punctuating bursts of baby talk—that had an embarrassingly private quality. Over his shoulder he said, "Good work." He then opened the grate and reached a hand inside. His arm made repetitive, gentle petting motions that filled me with relief.

"Excellent. Just excellent," he said. "This calls for a celebration, don't you think? Supper. Tomorrow. All of us. The Sky Club."

"Great. That sounds great," I said. "That sounds like fun." In his invitation I'd heard a hint that I could expect my payment during the meal, a setting more fitting than this one for such a ceremony. "What time?" I asked him.

"I'll ring you."

"That sounds great."

Clark grabbed hold of the handle on the pet crate. He tugged it to indicate that he wanted help but I was already on it, reaching over and taking upon myself the greater burden, because when I grasped the handle he eased off to the point of withdrawing his contribution. "I have the car waiting," he said. Followed by the recessive, spectral Sandra, we carried the crate outside through sliding doors and to a curb lined by limousines and vans and men holding hand-lettered signs with names on them. "Right here," he said. "This is perfect. This is splendid." We set the crate down and he turned to face me. He stuck one hand out, a fleshless, wan appendage with all the vitality seemingly bred out of it and fingers that appeared never to have worked other than to sign checks and dial phones. It wasn't clear to me which car was his, just that I'd not be riding in it with him to wherever he thought I might be going that night. I was staying at a friend's apartment, but Clark didn't know this because I hadn't told him. Other than how my flight had gone, he hadn't asked me a thing about myself. We said our goodbyes and I headed down the sidewalk to join a long line of people waiting for cabs. I didn't look back to watch him get into his car. I had an odd feeling he didn't want me to.

I SPENT THE NIGHT at the Greenwich Village apartment of my best friend from college, Douglas Rushkoff, a writer who called himself a "media theorist" and believed that computers and the Internet were changing us in ways we weren't aware of but that might prove transformative and magical. Or disastrous—he was still deciding. Doug, the son of a suburban accountant, was by far the smartest person I knew. In college we'd dabbled in mind-expanding chemicals and staged experimental, absurdist plays, our goal being to liberate ourselves from middle-class "consensus reality." We'd been at this project for fifteen years by then and were faring better than other classmates who'd aimed high artistically, panicked when they faltered, and settled, as we saw it, for dull careers in business. I depended on our conversations to form my opinions about technology, which was the great public subject at the moment. That night I could have used such a discussion to divert me from thinking about Clark and the extravagant favor I'd just done for him but had yet to be compensated for. Doug wasn't there, though. He was traveling, giving one of his speeches about the future.

Maggie was there. She'd flown in ahead of me; the delivery of Shelby represented a success for the animal shelter she headed up, which hoped that Clark would reward it with a generous donation. I told her about tomorrow's dinner plan and answered questions about my trip, downplaying its insults and its horrors, but I wasn't in a mood for intimacy.

In bed, as she slept, I allowed myself some optimism about the life awaiting me back home, which the trip had excused me from having to think about. I'd turn the job of remodeling the house over to a professional carpenter. I'd take a fresh look at a novel I'd abandoned and see if I couldn't finish it by fall, ship it off to my agent, and start another, possibly one that life might hand me if Clark and the muses cooperated. I'd refinance the ranch through a bank or mortgage company, retire my terrifying "contract for deed," replenish my savings through budgetary discipline, and climb back aboard the Dow Industrial Average—or the surging NASDAQ, even better. I'd also throw away the Ritalin, beginning with the bottle I had with me. By Christmas, God willing (Remember God, Walt? I'd grown up a Mormon and still tried to cut Him in on things, even though I'd left the church), the blur on the sonogram would be my daughter. It was time to prepare to hold her. To be a man.

WE MET CLARK AND Sandy for dinner at the Sky Club on the fifty-sixth floor of the MetLife building, the hulking *art brut* midtown office tower that arrogantly bisects Park Avenue. The club, with walls of windows on three sides and tables situated along its cliffs, was one of those overwhelming interior spaces that seem impossible until you're in them. Looking out from where we sat, buildings that seemed colossal from the street were revealed as marginal and secondary, their masts and spires petering out below us. I wasn't sure I liked the view. Not panoramic or comprehensive enough to stimulate meditative appreciation, it tickled the suicidal imagination, the part of the mind that pictures falls and leaps, with a beguiling specificity that forced me to withdraw my gaze lest my attention spin down into its depths.

"Is everything satisfactory?" Clark asked. His tone was jolly and proprietary. Indeed, he'd already pointed out to us that the dominant building in the vista—a limestone tower brushed by shafts of light shining upward from its base— belonged to "the family's place," Rockefeller Center. When he said this, I cut my eyes to Sandy, whose face masked a layer of spousal story fatigue that told me his stunt had been pulled before, and bored her.

Clark raised his glass: "To Shelby." We followed suit. She was down there somewhere with her wheelchair and her incontinence, submerged in the roaring grandeur of it all and possibly not equal to its pressures. Why had Clark wanted her so badly, courting the Pipers long distance through his computer practically every day, they'd said, for weeks? Her rarity, maybe. The rich prized rarities, not content with being rare themselves.

The food was forgettable but the conversation, once I gave myself to it and Clark got rolling, was like none I'd ever been a part of. Sandy, who'd heard much of it, presumably, busied herself with her silverware and napkin, while Maggie sat back as though attending a play, settling into her pregnant, hormonal fullness. First, came the peculiar personal tidbits. Clark, who'd ordered chicken for his meal, had never eaten a hamburger, he said, dined in a public restaurant, or tasted Coca-Cola. He asked me to describe its flavor, which flummoxed me. "Very sweet," I said. "And brown." Soon, he was relating his biography. As a child, he said, he'd suffered from aphasia, an inability to speak, but a chance encounter with a dog changed this when he was ten or so. He spoke the nonsense word "woofness" and recovered. A few years later, at just fourteen, he began attending Yale, his intelligence having unfolded at record speed once the magical animal untied his tongue.

The club workers came and went during this monologue, filling glasses and clearing plates, careful not to trespass on Clark's perimeter and hanging back whenever he grew animated. They called him "Sir" and "Mr. Rockefeller" and he directed their movements with amiable nods and glances.

The conversation shifted to public matters. Clark warned of a coming market crash, disclosing that the elites of the financial world had already set a date for the event and were positioning themselves accordingly. I asked what the date was. He said he didn't know, he only knew it had been agreed on recently. In anticipation of the debacle, he'd positioned himself in Treasuries, he said, and he cautioned me to do the same. Then he repeated his warnings about China and its expansive, imperial ambitions, using the term *Lebensraum* again, a word that seemed to please his vocal cords. Somehow he jumped from this to *Frasier*. He said he would be appearing on the show soon in the guise of a caller to the radio program hosted by the lead character, Dr. Crane, who advises people on the air about their psychiatric problems. Clark said he'd scripted his cameo himself. He'd play a caller with a compulsion to sing familiar songs from Broadway musicals in such a way that dog references and dog sounds were mixed in with the lyrics:

"The hills are alive with the bark of doggies, woof, woof, woof, woof, woof . . ."

Before I could absorb all this, Clark ever so discreetly slipped me what could only be my stipend, sealed in a long white business envelope. It happened without fanfare, at a moment when Sandra was engaged in cutting her food and Maggie was just returning from the bathroom. I declined to open the check in front of him, reluctant to commit a breach of protocol.

"What do you say we have some fun?" he said. He could tell I was having fun already. Gesturing toward the limestone monoliths looming in the window over his shoulder, he proposed an after-hours tour of Rockefeller Center, including certain subterranean sections inaccessible to the general public. He reached inside his jacket and patted something. "I happen to have it right here," he said. "The key."

"You have it?" I said. "You have the master key?" This assumed that there could be such an item, which seemed only reasonable, since there was such a thing as Clark. Maggie appeared to disagree. I glanced at her and caught a smirk on her freckled Irish face.

We ordered dessert, a slimy crème caramel with a brittle burnt-sugar cap, and the tour idea was shelved—maybe some other time, it was getting late. Clark buttoned his jacket and sat up in his chair and ate bites of custard lifted lightly on a fork. The windows in the buildings arrayed below us were lit up in broken diagonals and lines that spoke of a city in slowed-down weekend mode. A waiter approached and I ritually touched my wallet, but Clark waved me off. I never saw a check. Maybe private clubs delivered such bills at the end of the month, in the mail, all added up.

On the elevator ride back down, Clark invited me to his apartment the next day to see "the art." Could I come at noon? I could. "Fabulous. Fabulous," he said. My impression was that he did not consider the women essential to our emerging relationship.

At bedtime, I asked Maggie what she thought of him. She'd been notably silent on the subject.

"He puts on quite a show," she said. "I also think he might be gay."

"That's just the manner of those people."

"He doesn't listen, either. He just talks."

"What did you think of Sandy?"

"I'm not sure. She's quiet. He isn't very nice to her."

I didn't press her to say more. We had different investments in the matter and drawing attention to them seemed unwise, and probably unnecessary. We'd be home in a couple of days, with much in front of us. My odd new pal, if he continued to be a pal, would end up on my side of the ledger, along with the duties of housing, feeding, and clothing us. A thirteen-year age gap between a husband and wife, particularly when the wife works mostly at home and is only twenty-two, tends to promote certain very clear divisions. These existed in Clark's marriage, too, from what I'd seen of it—I just had no idea what they were.

WHEN I ARRIVED AT Clark's building the next day, prepared for a brush with Tony Bennett, the envelope with the check was still in my trouser pocket. Guessing at the sum was proving more stimulating than knowing it. An attendant showed me to an elevator, which let me out in a dim hallway behind whose doors I sensed no special wonders of decor or ornament. That rich people lived here didn't surprise me—I knew their preference for dull respectability— but it shocked me that a great singer would choose the place.

Clark's apartment was spare and unadorned—scuffed wood floors, a small dark sofa, a utilitarian kitchen with empty counters—but the art on the walls was bold and grand. It included a Mondrian in a Lucite box, a Motherwell, a Pollock, and a Rothko. I admired them, sipping a glass of water as we awaited the visit of a restorer from the Museum of Modern Art, which Clark said hoped to secure them for its collection. I couldn't help trying to estimate their value. Ten million? Twenty? It might be much, much more. A gentleman didn't ask such questions.

The apartment smelled stale and sour, not surprisingly,

like a kennel. Yates and Shelby were lying on the floor, giving each other jealous looks that seemed to portend a fight. Clark walked me over closer to the Pollock, which was leaning unframed against a wall, and picked something from its surface: a curly black dog hair.

"I believe that animals and art ought to coexist comfortably," he said. Then he showed me a smudge on the same painting. "Yates's saliva. He likes to lick," he said. "MoMA, of course, is utterly appalled. That's why they insist on weekly cleanings." He found another dog hair on the Mondrian, inside the Lucite box, and smiled. It seemed that his neglect of his collection made him prouder than the pieces themselves.

I complimented him on them anyhow. He told me they'd come to him partly by inheritance and partly through the efforts of a buyer—"a man I have in Spain"—who'd picked them up for a fraction of their value from certain cash-strapped European aristocrats and even a couple of renowned museums. He said I'd be shocked if he named these institutions. "It's rather scandalous," he said. The museums' directors were shady figures who'd needed to replace embezzled funds and Clark felt no guilt about exploiting them.

"One must never pass up a bargain," he concluded. "The irony is that I prefer Old Masters. Don't you agree?"

I nodded and said I did. It was baloney. I'd never considered the question. I'd definitely never considered it from the perspective of ownership.

I was starting to get hungry. I'd assumed on my way over that Clark would serve me lunch—after all, he had a chef—but there was no sign that a meal was in the offing, or even that meals were ever prepared here. An explanation arrived presently, possibly in response to some remark from me about the kitchen's extraordinary tidiness. Or maybe I said nothing. Maybe, as would happen often over the next few years, Clark read my mind.

"I have the identical apartment under this. It's where the help stays," he said. "They're off today." He looked at the floor as though he could see through it to the quarters below. I wondered where the entrance was, where the staircase came up—or weren't the places attached? Maybe you had to go out into the hall and take the elevator down.

The restorer rang the bell and Clark let him in while I knelt and calmed the dogs. The man unzipped a case of tools and brushes and went to work on the Pollock, ignoring us. Shelby seemed to have perked up since the trip and arched her neck against my hand as I stroked and scratched her. Clark, in an infantile, doggy voice, reassured a rivalrous-looking Yates that his place in the household wouldn't change because of his "new widdle sister." The dog voice saddened me. It seemed to convey Clark's lonely inner self more fully than his normal speaking voice, which wasn't all that normal. Given what he'd told us over dinner about his isolated, foreshortened childhood (Yale at fourteen couldn't have been easy), I realized that he was a largely self-nurtured being, a kind of waif or wolf boy, but with money. No wonder he loved animals.

The restorer packed his kit and left with a curt, no-eye-contact goodbye. I needed to eat. I felt a little dizzy. It was the summer of 1998 and unreality was in the air: a stock market buoyed by "irrational exuberance," a president in peril for lying about oral sex acts, and a heady profusion of new technologies with powers to reconfigure time and space. My new cell phone, temporarily quiet, was soon to mount an invasion of my consciousness that I had no way of imagining just then.

"How much do you know about Rothko's death?" Clark asked me. He invited me to look closely at the canvas, which he'd taken down from the wall. He turned it around and said something like, "He killed himself. He slit his wrists. On the back of this here, do you see these spots, these dribbles?"

I couldn't, but to please him I said I could. I'd traveled a ridiculously long way on an exhausting, humiliating errand, and I hoped we would be friends.

"It's blood," Clark said. "The artist's blood."

Down on the street, after I left his place, I opened the envelope. The check was drawn on his wife's account. Five hundred dollars. It didn't cover half of what I'd spent—and I still had to make the return trip. A mistake? Shouldn't the figure have another zero? Naturally, I never said a word.

FOUR

THE TRIAL OF Christian Karl Gerhartsreiter, a German immigrant of many aliases, for the 1985 murder of John Sohus in San Marino, California, began in early March 2013. It was held in downtown Los Angeles, in the Clara Shortridge Foltz Criminal Justice Center, a hulking, rectilinear, gray hive of offices and courtrooms that stands across a plaza from City Hall. It's a part of the city that's rarely seen on film—a district of dismal bureaucratic towers presiding over an outdoor homeless shelter. Attorneys, jurors, and city workers mix on the sidewalks with shopping-cart vagabonds and lean, shirtless drifters squatting in ragged camps. (One morning I saw a man hunched beside his bundle tending a pet brown rabbit on a leash.) The lawyers walk briskly past the squalid scene, jabbering into blinking Bluetooth headsets and sip-sucking Starbucks mochas through plastic cup lids. The jurors appear vaguely stranded and at loose ends, uprooted from their routines and livelihoods. Certain blocks are lined with parked police cars and media vans equipped with satellite masts. Most everyone who can leave by rush hour does.

On the first day of jury selection, I rode an elevator to the Foltz Center's metal detector–equipped ninth floor, the home of the city's highest-profile trials—O. J. Simpson, Phil Spector, Michael Jackson's doctor—and took a seat on a hard bench only a few feet away from the defendant. I had known him for almost fifteen years by then and considered him a friend for ten of them, visiting him at his clubs and in his homes, talking with him often on the phone, and casually tracking his passage toward middle age while keeping him informed of mine. Except at the very end of our relationship, after his divorce from Sandy, when he came to me bewildered by an experience that I'd endured myself a few years earlier, we were never close friends, never intimates, but he was a singular figure in my life and a subject of frequent contemplation. I'd never written about him as I'd planned—my literary killer instinct had yielded to a desire for his favor—but I nevertheless imagined I'd understood him. Events had proved me wrong. They'd proved a lot of people wrong.

He was dressed the way he had been when I'd known

him, as Clark Rockefeller (the name he also used with his attorneys and fruitlessly asked the court to recognize), in a preppy blue blazer, gray slacks, and a white shirt, every item a size too big. He still wore shoes without socks, exposing pale gaps of ankle, but he'd traded the thick black glasses I used to see him in for a professorial rimless pair. His hair had darkened to a mousy brown and his face was leaner than in the past, which emphasized the sharpness of his long nose and the elfin points of his big ears. According to the German passport found by investigators in a hiding place where he'd stashed various personal belongings, including several paintings rolled up in tubes and a book of signed blank checks from Sandy, whose salary had helped bankroll his charade, he had just turned fifty-two years old.

He'd been in prison for four years by then, the result of a prior conviction in Massachusetts for abducting his daughter, whom he called "Snooks," in 2008, during a supervised visit in Boston. I'd met her in 2002, when she was one, during a visit to his rambling country house in Cornish, New Hampshire. He'd lured me there with a promise to introduce me to J. D. Salinger, who lived nearby and was, Clark said, a friend. Later on in the trial that mad weekend would come back to me, reemerging in hindsight as the moment when all the clues were spread out for me to read and I should have caught him at his game, but for now my clearest memory was the child. She was learning to walk, I remembered. She stuck her arms out, toddling unsteadily toward a sofa where he sat coaching her, saying, "Snooks can do it." Sandy, who'd just returned from a long business trip, stood by looking haggard and angry. The child made the crossing. People clapped.

Clark snatched her when she was seven, off the street, bundling her into a hired SUV whose driver had been made to think that the pursuing social worker—who grabbed the car door and was thrown aside—was Clark's obsessed gay stalker. Several blocks on, Clark had the driver stop and caught a cab to a prearranged location where another dupe, a female friend, was waiting to drive him to New York City, supposedly to meet a yacht. (He paid her five hundred dollars for her services, apparently his customary rate.) From there, he and Snooks proceeded by unknown means to a house he'd bought in Baltimore, where he'd spent months preparing a new identity under the blandest of all his phony names: Chip Smith.

What he planned for his next move wasn't known; after a nationwide four-day manhunt FBI agents tracked him to the house and lured him outside with a staged phone call in which he was told that a catamaran he'd purchased was taking on water in the harbor. I had reason to think from a conversation we'd had a few months before the crime that he might have been headed for Peru, a country which he'd told me refused to extradite American parents who fled there with their children. This tidbit came up during one of the long phone calls that followed his divorce, when Clark would rant about Sandy's "cruelty" in separating him from Snooks. I was a divorced father myself by then and

I sympathized with his frustrations, but now and then his intensity alarmed me. His mention of Peru as a safe haven was part of a troublingly transparent probe into my own potential willingness to act extremely in custody matters. Clark believed that the American legal system shamefully disregards the rights of fathers and that, as its victims, we needed to fight back.

The kidnapping, which made international news and later inspired a TV movie, exposed Clark Rockefeller as a fraud, the most prodigious serial impostor in recent history. It also connected him to a lineage older, and in a certain fashion richer, than that of the founding family of Standard Oil: the shape-shifting trickster of American myth and literature. In Melville's *The Confidence-Man: His Masquerade*, this figure takes the form of a mutating devil aboard a riverboat who feeds on his fellow passengers' moral defects. In *Hucklebery Finn*, he again stalks the Mississippi River as the Duke and the Dauphin, flamboyant mock aristocrats whose swindles are cloaked in Elizabethan claptrap. In *The Great Gatsby* he's a preening gangster sprouted from a North Dakota farm boy. In Patricia Highsmith's *Ripley* novels he's a murderous social-climbing dilettante. In Joseph Heller's *Catch-22* he's Milo Minderbinder, the blithe wheeler-dealer who'd blow up the world if he saw a profit in it. He's the villain with a thousand faces, a kind of charming, dark-side cowboy, perennially slipping off into the sunset and reappearing at dawn in a new outfit.

But if Clark was all that (I'd learn after the trial that he understood his literary provenance and took great pride in it), then what was I? A fool. A stubborn fool. When his story began to unravel during the manhunt, and the Rockefellers claimed not to know him, I told a fellow reporter that they were lying, a family of cowards running from a scandal. I only backed down when his German name was published and the word *Lebensraum* echoed through my head. The disclosure unsettled me but it also softened me, especially when more facts about his background trickled out in the days after his capture. I too had a German name and German blood, and I'd spent a summer during college living in Bavaria, his home province. I was eighteen then, about the same age he was when, in 1979, two years before my stay in Munich, he left the small town of his youth for the United States. I'd left my own small town that year, for Princeton. I knew the yearning. No wonder we'd been friends.

This state of befuddled recognition ended when it was reported a couple of weeks after the kidnapping that Clark (the name Christian would never fit the slot; it lacked the snap I associated with him) had been linked through his fingerprints to a certain Christopher Chichester, who was wanted for questioning in a cold-case murder. The grisly particulars of the crime unnerved me: in 1985, John Sohus's corpse had been dismembered and buried in his mother's yard, where his bones were unearthed nine years later by swimming-pool excavators. Linda Sohus, the victim's wife, had vanished at the same time as her husband. Her body had never been recovered. Nor had police been able to locate

Chichester, who'd been living on the property in a guest-house rented from Sohus's mother.

HEARING ALL THIS, AND then seeing Chichester's picture—it was a younger Clark in a tie and jacket, looking sly, with a one-step-ahead-of-all-of-you expression—I recalled a fuss he'd made once about his aversion to the sight of blood. It jellied his knees. It made his head swim. Like much that he said, the remarks came out of nowhere, unprompted and seemingly without a motive, just more of the colorful fog he spread around himself in what I'd diagnosed by then as a mild case of logorrhea, the compulsion to soothe oneself with talk, talk, talk.

On the day I relinquished my cell phone, keys, and wallet to the Foltz Center's hypersensitive metal detector, the shock of Clark's unmasking had not worn off. If anything, it had deepened over the years, combining with and compounding all the other shocks that I'd suffered since befriending him. The first, most savage of these traumas—the one that somehow stood for all the rest—occurred on the ranch, the day after my fortieth birthday. I was sitting in my blue Ford pickup, the one that killed Miles and helped deliver Shelby. I was idling in the driveway near the house, about to fetch some hay bales from a field. Standing beside me at the driver's-side window was a friend from New York who'd flown out to help me celebrate. We spoke a few words as I put the truck in gear, and just as it rolled forward on its big tires, my friend cast a glance at the ground directly in front of me, a spot I couldn't see below the hood, and hollered, "Charlie!," the name of my one-year-old, who loved to crawl. The truck rolled on, a good ten feet—momentum. I stopped it as time elongated and yawned and I became a speck or cinder drifting in a nauseating gray void. I shifted into Park. I climbed down from the cab. Life had just ended for me, so I was calm. I hurried, because one must, but I was calm. With forty more years to absorb the ghastly image already taking shape in my mind's eye, adrenaline and panic were irrelevant.

He was sitting upright under the license plate, halfway between the rear tires. My perfect boy. The pickup's jacked-up, four-wheel-drive suspension had allowed the chassis to pass right over him. It made no sense. The overlay of horror—the scene that should have been—persisted in my vision as I reached for him. Angels. Providence. Only they made sense. In the realm of logic and causality, I'd killed my child, but love had vanquished physics and here he was in my arms, against my chest, with nothing but a pink patch on his forehead where the truck's differential had scraped the skin.

The accident sent a tremor through my life. Two years later I was divorced. I worked too hard. We'd never been a match. Mercury was in retrograde. Things change. Compared to what else can happen in this world, and to what almost had the day after my birthday, the divorce felt like business, a sad adult procedure. I'd married a teenager, what did I expect? To be the exception, as usual. Guess not. The sentimental turns to the statistical. I hung on to the ranch for a time, which seemed important, but cash ran low and I sold it to a neighbor who happened to be a real estate agent. A few days later he resold the place to a wealthy buyer he'd had waiting, pocketing a nice margin.

I saw my children—Charlie, and his older sister, Maisie— every other weekend, a schedule that makes a flip-card movie of parenthood. Sometimes they grew half an inch between our visits. I filled in the downtime with girlfriends and magazine work and wishful spasms of gym activity. Men who live alone don't live originally. We eat at the bar. We file for tax extensions. We call our worried mothers too often, no longer to spring exciting news on them—that season is over, and perhaps not missed—but to replay a skirmish with the ex-wife or get advice on what to tell a child who's been caught viewing hard-core Internet pornography. It's better, we think, than not calling her at all, and she must think so too, since she picks up.

Then one day she doesn't. In the summer of 2011, after a month of mysterious chills and headaches that she self-diagnosed as Lyme disease and treated with Excedrin and doxycycline, my mother died of an abscess of the brain. She was only seventy-one. She collapsed at her boyfriend's house in Iowa after a three-day visit to the State Fair. Her last meal was a snow cone. She lingered in a coma long enough for me to reach her bedside in Des Moines and, in the spirit of the living will that she kept folded in her purse, consent to the morphine drip that eased her passage. Because someone had told me the sense of hearing goes last, I held my phone beside her pillow and played her Bob Dylan's "I Shall Be Released." A day later, I drove to her house in Minnesota. In the center of her kitchen table, clipped in one of those little wire stands that florists put in bouquets to hold a card, was a note listing bank account numbers and names of lawyers. It was headed "If I die."

The cumulative result of all these shocks was to deplete some reserve of basic courage that I'd taken for granted since childhood. I wasn't so much depressed as chronically hesitant. Simple decisions that I'd once made thoughtlessly—whether to ask a woman on a date, whether to leave a front door key with a plumber, whether to answer a phone call from a strange number—felt loaded with uncertainty and peril. It didn't help any that out in Massachusetts, and then in California, my old friend Clark, under a foreign name, was wending his way through the criminal justice system, first for a crime he'd committed while I'd known him and that I hadn't seen coming but probably should have, and then for an older, more abhorrent offense that, the more I thought about our friendship, seemed coiled inside our interactions like a tiny, embryonic snake.

"Hitler went to heaven."

"The artist's blood."

I hadn't known him. I'd misinterpreted everything. Though it wasn't the harshest blow of the last decade, it may have been the most destabilizing, undermining my trust in other people and devastating my faith in my own judgment. Qualities in myself that I'd thought laudable—curiosity, openness, high spirits—suddenly felt like shortcomings or defects. "You can't cheat an honest man" goes the old saying, the notion being that falling for a charlatan requires moral softness in the victim. I had plenty of this, as I was well aware thanks to my upbring-ing in the Mormon Church. I lied on occasion, chiefly about sex. I could be two-faced around authority figures, kissing up to them while resenting them. At times I relished speaking caustically. And what I regarded as my trusting nature was, upon inspection, a kind of sloth. Instead of patiently working to get to know people, I'd decide that they were who I wanted them to be and discard them when they proved otherwise. This cycle of disappointment happened often. That it hadn't come close to happening with Clark—that he never diverged from my fantasies about him—should have been a sign.

Another symptom of my spiritual laxity was the Ritalin I was taking when I knew him. Its effect was to grant me cheap energy on cue, and thanks to the way I was living and working then—juggling deadlines, ranch chores, and young children—my demand for cheap energy was vast. The cycles of euphoria and exhaustion induced by the drug caused many skids and stumbles. I squandered thousands on online trading sprees. Buy Lucent Technologies at 28, sell in a sweat when it dips to 26, rebuy at 27, watch it rise, double up when it spikes, freak out when it ticks down, sell half, sell all, buy Apple, and on and on. I ordered a car once in this scrambled state, leaning in next to the salesman at his computer and choosing options that showed up on his screen as a morphing animated vehicle that kept changing colors because I couldn't pick one. Maybe the pills were one reason I bought Clark. The mood of promiscuous readiness they roused was indiscriminate and undiscerning.

Or maybe my egotism was a homing beacon. Maybe it made me a more attractive mark. Our history ran both ways, a partnership, meaning that whatever I'd seen in him, he had also spied something in me. These characters read you, according to the books, and all the time they're talking, they're really listening, alert for pings and echoes. They use sonar, not questions; Clark never asked me questions. I suspect that one quality he tuned in to early on was my collaborative listening style. Instead of shrinking from his loopy stories, I helped him refine them by teasing out their details and nudging them toward heightened vividness. It's one of the services Nick performs for Gatsby, consolidating his fabricated self by playing the role of ideal audience.

Clark would also have felt my eagerness not only to trust but to be trusted. He'd told me in our initial phone call that his plane was in China with his wife, and yet there she was when I arrived with Shelby. I don't recall him explaining this inconsistency. I do recall noting it and saying nothing. What is it in people, or just in people like me, that would rather let a lie go by, would rather wish it away or minimize it, than point it out and cause the liar embarassment? Why would we rather have someone see us naked than see someone naked? Politeness, I'd always thought. The essence of politeness is feigned blindness. But Clark knew otherwise.

He knew that my choice to spare him the slightest shame, to view him as he wanted to be viewed, stemmed from a selfish craving for an alliance. I would blink when he stumbled, go deaf when he misspoke. He could count on me.

I'd come to Clark's murder trial with many questions, beginning with why I'd once found him so impressive and how, in instance after instance—some of them still in the process of resurfacing—I could have been so stupid, so obtuse. I also wanted to learn how his pretensions might be related to a violent nature (if Clark even had a "nature," a larger question). But there was this, too: I'd come to finish a story, the one I'd considered writing when I met him but later abandoned in deference to our friendship.

I still remembered where I was when I ruled out using him as a character, even in fiction. The Lotos Club on East 66th Street is a quietly posh refuge for Manhattan's cultural elites. Mark Twain was once a member. He called it "the ace of clubs." Its manicured furnishings and forgiving lighting brought to mind an exquisite funeral home or a faculty club for learned ghosts. We sat in high-backed chairs that afternoon, the focus of a grudging, aging staff whose loathing for us was obvious. He was drinking a gin and tonic. I had a Coke with lemon. I don't recall the topics we discussed, but they probably touched on global politics and his arch-theme of Western decadence versus Asian drive and discipline. Behind his chair was a portrait of some dead worthy gazing immortally into a future that the man appeared confident of shaping. Perhaps he had; I didn't recognize him. My hunch was that this would not have bothered him, since men of true influence operate offstage.

I wanted to be invited back—I liked the club's effect on me. I liked how it made me hold my glass, not wrapped in my hand and snug against my palm the way I'd hold it in a restaurant but lightly, with precise, prehensile fingertips. I also liked how comfortable I felt, sitting askew on my cushion, head tipped sideways, thumb on cheekbone, ankles crossed, mirroring the flow of Clark's remarks with adjustments of forehead tension and chin position. I wasn't the lone Princetonian there, I sensed. I doubted that I was the lone Oxfordian, either. Was that my old roommate's father in the striped tie? The wrinkles across the insteps of his brogues were exactly the ones I wanted on mine someday. Montana—I may have erred there. Too far afield. Perhaps it was time to move back to the center. ("I think you nailed it, Clark. I really do. I suspect that's what most people think but never say.") We made an interesting pair, the small-town novelist and the lonesome Rockefeller. I brought him news of the people, the human ruckus, and he brought me news from the Olympian eagle's nest. ("I think I'll switch to club soda with a lime. And you can take these nuts. We're done.") He envied my mobility, my freedom; I coveted his security, his ease. What was funny was how protective I felt toward him. What was nice was how safe he seemed to feel with me.

These memories struck me as absurd now, a ridiculous, disgraceful capitulation. I'd bowed to a tinfoil prince. I'd kissed his ring, and the irony was that the true ring was on my hand.

The only Ivy Leaguer there was me. The only Lotos Club type was sitting in my chair. I'd had it all backwards, upside down, reversed. I, the fawning aspirant, should have been the one conferring status—and I suppose I was, in some sick way. Clark must have loved it, watching me degrade myself. Worse, though, I was degrading my vocation. My grant of literary immunity to the strangest creature I'd ever met violated my storyteller's oath. Writers exist to exploit such figures, not to save them. Our duty is to the page, not the person.

The trial was my chance to right all this, to call off a deal I shouldn't have agreed to and hadn't been asked to agree to, come to think of it. I'd made the deal unilaterally, with myself, hoping that he'd reward my generosity. No more of that. The trial meant Clark's story was reaching a conclusion; if I hoped to catch up with it and make sense of it by exploring its intersections with mine, the time was now, the place was here. Two basic outcomes were possible, and two morals. If Clark were found guilty, Abe Lincoln would be proved right—you can't fool all the people all the time—and I would be present to savor his comeuppance and participate in my own redemption. If he were found innocent, however, the tale would end on a warped, postmodern note, and Clark might well emerge as a celebrity, proving the world was a bigger dupe than me. I felt prepared for both contingencies, but I feared that the second, limbo, was more likely.

The name of the case seemed to foreordain a muddle: "The People of the State of California, Plaintiff, vs. Christian K. Gerhartsreiter, aka Christopher Chichester, aka Christopher

Crowe, aka C. Crowe Mountbatten, aka Clark Rockefeller, aka Charles 'Chip' Smith." The nature of the jury concerned me too. Its members would be drawn from the same neighborhoods that supplied the bumbling O. J. Simpson jury. The word from the old hands around the courthouse was that downtown LA jurors shared a reflexive suspicion of authority and a frank dislike for the police. I'd also heard rumors of their scorn for circumstantial evidence, which TV crime shows supposedly had taught them was inferior to smoking-gun stuff such as trace DNA and microscopic fibers. If indeed this prejudice existed, it would favor the defense; I happened to know from pretrial publicity that circumstantial evidence—really just an incriminating story about Clark's peculiar behavior before the murder and his evasive behavior afterward—was almost all the prosecution had.

The process of choosing this jury went on all day. Waiting in the hallway outside the courtroom, the pool of a few dozen prospects blended well with the associates of local gang lords whose trials were taking place in the same building. Not one of the candidates resembled Clark or someone he might have relaxed with at the Lotos Club, but many of them had the class and ethnic markers of "service people," the folks he'd probably engaged as cleaners and gardeners. The euphemism that sprang to mind was "urban." One middle-aged Latino man with a lordly stomach, a curled, waxed mustache with twisted points, and a sizable tattoo partially visible above his collarline, wore his straw hat and dark shades into the courtroom when the bailiff called his name. "Clark's defense will definitely want that guy," whispered Frank Girardot, the editor of the *Pasadena Star News* and a veteran trial reporter who'd covered the Simpson case. Girardot was right; the big fellow made the cut.

Judge George Lomeli worked his way through the long procession of candidates, many of whom spoke halting English, while others seemed past their prime as alert, analytic intellects. Lomeli appeared well-suited for the case, a handsome man with a sharp but genial manner that combined authority and wit and even a hint of debonair Old Hollywood. He looked good in his robe, which matched his hair and mustache, and he appealed to the candidates' sporting sides by promising an "interesting" trial. Lots of folks tried to beg off anyway, citing work conflicts, family difficulties, and religious holidays. Of those who seemed most inclined to do their duty, some appeared to have little else going on. This bothered me. If I, the Princeton and Oxford graduate, had fallen for Clark's ingenious stratagems, how would these people penetrate the veil? With some jurors, I feared a culture clash. I'd seen a list of the prosecution's witnesses, among whom were several white-shoe finance types who'd known Clark in his late-1980s guise as Christopher Crowe, a hungry Wall Street bond guy. The working-class jurors might find these smoothies baffling, or loathe them on sight. Would it matter? No idea. I'd never attended a murder trial before. I'd certainly never had a stake in one.

My stake in this one was hard to formulate. The harm Clark had caused me wasn't grave enough to instill a lust for vengeance, but I hardly wished him well. The murder aside, he had a lot to answer for, and the trial was likely to offer him many rebukes, even if it spared him the ultimate one. Gratifying and fascinating viewing. I hoped my time here would educate me, toughen me. Having been beguiled by his magic show, I would now be able to go backstage and see the tricks he'd played explained. "That Walter Kirn is one shrewd judge of character"—this had never been said of me. Maybe the trial would wake me up.

As the potential jurors faced the judge, Clark turned around and watched them from his chair. Now and then he'd offer them sad smiles, affecting sympathy for their complaints, but mostly he wore the detached, attentive look of an anthropologist in the field. Who *were* all these people, so many of them *so* brown? What *was* this ritual unfolding around him? I'd never seen a German look as German as Clark did when he assessed his likely assessors. His eyes were like small blue coins behind his glasses. One sockless foot tapped away beneath his chair. In his right hand he held a pencil stub poised above a yellow legal pad. I'd heard he'd been writing a novel while in prison, a multipart epic of European politics that began at the close of World War One and ended in the 1960s. It was competent but dull, I'd heard, well researched but inert.

That Clark was guilty I had little doubt. Twenty-eight years ago, here in California, he'd killed his landlady's adopted son and his life ever since had been a masquerade. The trial would permit the prosecution to color in and substantiate this story, but I already knew it in outline and found it credible. What I didn't find credible anymore was me. When I'd learned that Clark might be a murderer and instinctively found the notion plausible, the effect on me was Galilean. It humbled me. It reoriented everything. It revealed to me the size and power of my ignorance and vanity.

About two hours into jury selection, while scrutinizing another would-be juror, Clark glanced to the side and saw me sitting there. I nodded at him. I thought he might nod back. I was, after all, a face from better days. He sneered at me instead, arching his eyebrows, wrinkling his nose, and twisting up his lips into a horrible, prissy little knot. The look was vicious and contemptuous and indicated that he viewed my presence as a betrayal of our relationship, as conduct unbecoming a gentleman. I viewed things differently, of course. To me our relationship was the betrayal. Nor did I care anymore to be a gentleman.

For the rest of his trial, until we met again, he pretended that I wasn't there.

FIVE

CHRISTOPHER CHICHESTER WAS a baronet, a species of minor British aristocrat. It said so on the vellum card that he passed out at church socials and Rotary meetings, a card that also bore a Latin motto whose English translation—if anyone cared to check—was "Firm in Faith." He told people that he was distantly related to Sir Francis Chichester, a figure of lofty nautical renown who'd circled the globe on a sailboat, the *Gipsy Moth*. In what would become a lifelong habit of claiming involvement with whichever movies happened to be foremost in the headlines, he also told people that he knew George Lucas, the creator of *Star Wars*.

It was the early 1980s, around the time I was studying at Oxford with actual English nobles, and America was rekindling its romance with hierarchy and pedigree and pomp after a long spell of earthy, druggy populism. Not that stuffy San Marino, a wealthy enclave near Pasadena settled by General George S. Patton's grandfather, had ever fallen for the hippie gospel. The town was a fanciful fortress for the privileged whose houses aped, with that California fondness for the air-conditioned copy over the poorly ventilated original, Tudor manors, French chateaus, and other overbearing Old World domiciles. Its shade trees were prodigies of photosynthesis, a smog-scrubbing, heat-shielding canopy of verdure. The cars in its driveways were showroom glossy. The Chandlers lived there. They published the *LA Times*. John McCone lived there. He'd run the CIA once. The Huntington Library, founded by a railroad baron, held one of only eleven existing vellum copies of the Gutenberg Bible, several quarto editions of *Hamlet*, and perhaps the world's finest collection of eighteenth-century British portrait art, including Thomas Gainsborough's *The Blue Boy*.

Chichester had found his Oz, his Xanadu, and his West Egg. He'd come a long way, and by a zigzag route. The son of a housepainter and a part-time seamstress, he'd grown up in Roman Catholic rural Bavaria in a village called Bergen, the German equivalent of those stifling small American towns in country western songs. The locals remembered him as bright, dissatisfied, infatuated with Hollywood, and rude—a child who once blew pepper into a teacher's face and was given to picking fights. In an article in the *Boston Globe* that ran after the kidnapping of Snooks, his younger brother, Alexander, said: "I think Germany was too small for him. He wanted to live in the big country and maybe get famous." Out hitchhiking one stormy day, he caught a ride with a couple on vacation, a California dentist and his wife, whom he thought might aid him in his plan. He invited them home to eat dinner with his family and pumped them for information about America. Just days or weeks later he called them on the phone and announced that he'd made the crossing.

The gateway he chose was Berlin, Connecticut, perhaps because it rang a bell. Through an advertisement in the paper, he found a local family that was willing to host a foreign exchange student. He enrolled in high school. He told people that his father was an industrialist and set about fashioning a manner based on a pop-culture travesty of wealth: Thurston Howell III of *Gilligan's Island*, one of his favorite television shows. When his host family tired of his peculiar pretensions, he skipped off to Wisconsin and settled in Milwaukee, a city of breweries and bratwurst and an appropriate haven for a young German who was still in the process of denaturalizing himself. He studied communications at a local state university. He shortened his last name to "Gerhart." He arranged a quickie marriage for a green card. Ready for another leap, he ditched his new wife and friends and his old name and lit out for California.

There, he burrowed into the white side of Los Angeles, up against the mountains. South Pasadena was his entry point,

specifically its Episcopal church, St. James. He understood
the power of God as a character reference. He ushered on
Sundays, cultivated the priest, and rented a series of lodgings
from parishioners, never lasting long in any one place. He
claimed to be studying film at USC and blamed stingy parents for his lack of funds. He moved up the ladder of zip codes
to San Marino and leased a backyard guesthouse from Didi
Sohus, a lonesome woman in late middle age who drank and
smoked and drank and smoked and failed to maintain her
yard and drank and smoked. Didi's type—propertied, isolated, out of it—was a type that his type prized.

How he paid the rent has never been clear. After his trial,
when we finally met again, he would feed me a story about
importing tea directly from Asia, from a grand estate, and
peddling it to churches and VFW halls, but I had no more
reason to believe this than his neighbors in California did
when he told them he owned a talking car. (*Knight Rider*,
a TV show of the period, happened to feature just such a
verbal vehicle.) What is known, however, is how he paid for
meals. He didn't. He'd post himself at the local barbershop,
Jann of Sweden, and listen in on customers—among them
the Chandler men on whose conservative haircuts he mod-
eled his own—while drinking free coffee and browsing the
free papers. At the right moment, he'd comment or ask a
question, slipping into the stream of conversation. An invitation to lunch or breakfast might follow. He'd accept. When
the bill arrived, no wallet. He hadn't been planning to eat.
He'd get it next time. Perpetual postponement became his

method. He thrived in the gap between actions and their consequences, concealment and discovery.

"He didn't know much," Jann told me after court one day, "but he knew enough to make people think he did."

The baronet didn't deign to speak to everyone. One person he ignored, by most accounts, was geeky John Sohus, then in his mid-twenties. John, who lived with his mother in the main house, was diabetic and adopted. He played Dungeons and Dragons. He loved Tolkien. He knew how to program an Apple II computer back when such knowledge was not a route to millions but a pursuit whose prestige among his peer group lay somewhere between thumbsucking and juggling. John was a little guy. His girlfriend, Linda, who worked in a San Fernando Valley fantasy bookstore, Dangerous Visions, had a good six inches and fifty pounds on him. Her hobby was painting unicorns and centaurs; she hoped to make a career of it someday. For their wedding, the couple threw a costume party—one guest was a robot, another a horned demon—and held it on a doubly spooky date: Halloween, 1984.

A few months later, the prosecution charged, the film student who wasn't enrolled in film school and didn't appear to be flourishing in Hollywood despite his supposed connections to top directors, bashed in John's skull with three blows from a blunt object and stabbed him repeatedly in the back and arms with something razor-like and piercing. No motive for the crime was given in court (California law does not require one), but it may have involved a modest inheritance destined for John that Chichester coveted. Detectives would later interview a woman from whom he extracted, the woman said, a forty-thousand-dollar "'finder's fee" for her right to nurse an ailing Didi, who felt abandoned by her missing son. In 1987, with John still gone, Didi put the woman in her will and perished soon afterward while in her care. Chichester showed up to split the take but there wasn't much left, the woman told police, and she sent him away unsatisfied. The story was inadmissable in court because the night before the woman was set to be formally deposed, she died.

So Chichester may have killed John Sohus for nothing. He may also have done the following for nothing:

Cut the body up into three sections, possibly with an electric chain saw he borrowed from a neighbor around this time.

Placed the head inside two plastic shopping bags, both of them from college bookstores, one at the University of Wisconsin, Milwaukee, the other at USC.

Wrapped the hands in plastic grocery bags.

Wound the torso in plastic sheets.

Dug a three-foot-deep pit in the backyard, stuffed at least a portion of the remains into a fiberglass drum, and buried them. Wiped up the blood in the guesthouse and burned the carpet.

Returned the chain saw. Arranged to have forwarded from France a series of postcards written either by Linda or by a forger familiar with her handwriting—possibly the baronet himself—informing her mother-in-law and several friends that she and John were enjoying a holiday abroad.

But Linda wasn't in Europe. She was gone. She never returned to work at Dangerous Visions. She never answered the phone calls from the man who'd bought a couple of her paintings—her first sale!—and she never drove out to Phoenix with her best friend for the big science fiction and fantasy convention that they'd been planning to attend. She also missed the little garden party that Chichester organized a few months later, setting up a table in the backyard next to the dirt mound atop her husband's grave.

Linda, whose new white Nissan pickup truck Chichester then drove back to the East Coast, where all the dog-loving freelance central bankers live.

TWO NIGHTS BEFORE THE trial proper began I slept in my car in a drugstore parking lot somewhere between the airport and downtown. I'd driven into the city from Malibu, where I was renting a studio apartment, to talk about the murder over dinner with a new friend, the novelist James Ellroy, author of *LA Confidential*, who viewed Clark as a stone psychopath. I missed my exit and wound up on a freeway—not the one I'd driven in on—cruising along through the dark with my attention fixed on the map application on my phone, which represented my car as a blue dot and my destination, a restaurant, as a red dot. For what I believed was twenty minutes but was actually an hour, I followed the dot instead of heeding the road signs, only realizing how lost I was when I reached a potholed dead-end street in a deserted warehouse district. Because Ellroy didn't own a cell phone, I had to call the restaurant and ask for him. I described my location to him using landmarks, having turned off the phone app in disgust. "You're not even in Los Angeles," he said. "You're way down in San Pedro. You fucked up."

I told him to eat without me. Then my phone died. I tried to retrace my route from memory. Around midnight, I bought a map at a convenience store that looked like it was robbed weekly by armed junkies but carried on selling Red Bull and Camels anyway. Ninety minutes of driving, I discovered, had returned me to San Pedro. I gave up then—fatigue and urban sprawl had beaten me. My pillow was a rolled-up leather jacket. At four A.M. I woke up in a panic, convinced that Clark would go free after the trial and come for me somehow, possibly in disguise. Then I remembered the dream that spurred this thought. A police car had pulled me over on a dirt road and I was waiting to show my driver's license to an officer who I could see approaching in my rearview mirror. His body grew larger with each step but his head kept shrinking. By the time he reached the car he had no head. He had a voice, however: Clark's. He asked me for my ID and I woke up.

Behind the dream was a bad memory that I'd been living with for years, ever since I learned about the murder charge. It was late October 1998, a few months after I delivered Shelby. I opened an e-mail at my desk—a group e-mail to multiple recipients that included the Pipers—in which Clark described a nervous breakdown he'd suffered while supposedly attending a meeting at the United Nations. He blamed the pressures of his banking job. He blamed the demands of caring for a sick dog, who woke early, cutting short his sleep. Under a doctor's orders to change his lifestyle, he planned to close his office and "go virtual" the following spring. He also mentioned a planned sabbatical. "I may either stay at a friend's summerhouse in the Brittany/Normandy region," he wrote, "or even visit Shelby's former home state, Montana."

This sentence jarred me. I couldn't imagine a graver mismatch than Clark and Big Sky country. He couldn't be serious. I wondered if the plan involved the Pipers, with whom I'd fallen out of touch as I prepared for Maggie's November due date.

The birth of my daughter, Maisie, a few weeks later pushed Clark and his e-mail from my mind. The morning after Maggie delivered her, a red, roaring baby who barreled into the world with a momentum still present fourteen years later, my agent sold a novel of mine that seventeen different publishers had passed on. Over the next month, on instructions from my new editor, I revised it at night in my unfinished kitchen, sitting on the floor with my computer perched on a five-gallon bucket of drywall compound. So Maggie could sleep, I laid Maisie in a laundry basket and watched her while I typed. It startled me every time I met her eyes, which still had the undifferentiated composure of small blue portals to another galaxy. They recognized everything and nothing. Their pupils were perfect black unblinking Buddhas.

At some point during this interlude Clark called. He opened with his accustomed greeting: "Long time, no speak."

(Most of his pet colloquialisms were like this—variations on familiar sayings that weren't as witty as he seemed to think.) After I brought him current on my news, he retold the story of his breakdown, giving special attention to his lapse into unconsciousness and to his intention to rest up as he wound down his banking consultancy, which restructured Third World debt and strove to reinvigorate whole national economies whose ailments were untreatable, he feared.

"Next summer I might like to stay with you," he said. "I think Montana might just do the trick for me."

"Stay with me?"

"On your ranch," he said. "While I look for a property of my own to buy. I've got the Pipers on the job."

I told him "No." I said it wouldn't work. My refusal was automatic and unyielding. He tried to soften me by playing up his troubling nervous symptoms. He even brought Shelby into it, describing a fight she'd had in Central Park with another dog whose owners were suing him. She had nowhere to roam now, but Montana would solve this problem. "Impossible," I said. I cited my baby. I cited lack of space. He answered that he didn't need space. Did I own a garage? He could live in my garage. I said, "You're joking." He said he wasn't. He said that he'd lived in a tiny guesthouse once, a single room with nothing but a bed, and had never been happier in all his life.

THE DEPUTY DISTRICT ATTORNEY trying the case, Habib Balian, was a gangly, sweet-faced fellow with a long nose and animated, double-jointed hands. His manner was fetchingly boyish and distracted, causing Judge Lomeli to compare him, in what became a trial-long running joke, to the rumpled TV sleuth Columbo. For literate court watchers, this joke had punch, since Columbo was a modern homage to Inspector Porfiry in *Crime and Punishment*. He traps Raskolnikov in a cat-and-mouse game after the murder of a pawnbroker by toying with the accused's half-conscious urge to confess obliquely to the killing through strange, self-sabotaging acts at odds with his arrogant intention to commit the "perfect crime." To me Balian also resembled, physically, a young Armenian Lincoln.

During his opening statement, which ran all morning and was interrupted by a lunch break, Balian sometimes had trouble working the computer that let him show PowerPoint projections of photos, diagrams, and other evidence. Among the first slides that he put up were shots of John Sohus's skeletal remains, both in the form that the swimming-pool diggers found them—bagged and wrapped and scattered in the pit—and as the coroner reassembled them. The pictures were dingy and confusing. The remains looked like pieces of garbage, like scraps of trash. They shocked me at first but I soon grew used to them. What I didn't grow used to was the strenuous stage squint that Clark affected when he viewed them. I interpreted the expression as his answer to a highly specialized challenge: how to seem concerned about a dead man whom one has been charged with killing and dismembering without appearing *personally* concerned.

Balian used the computer again after the lunch break. He'd reached the climax of his narrative about the defendant's elaborate life of fakery in the decades between the murder and his capture. Though the court had forbidden any overt mentions of the kidnapping of little Snooks, Balian was permitted to show a clip of Clark's bizarre appearance on the *Today* show shortly after his arrest in Baltimore.

"All right, so in 2008," said Balian, looking at the screen, which displayed an image of a red-haired Clark wearing his chunky clear-lensed Ray-Ban Wayfarers and sitting across from a female interviewer, "the defendant went on national TV. He is still trying to convince everyone that he was not Christian Gerhartsreiter, and he was asked, 'Did you kill John and Linda Sohus,' and you'll see what he says. First he's asked who he is."

The tape:

"Is there a real name that we should be calling you?"

"Clark Rockefeller."

"Clark Rockefeller, you say, is still your real name?"

"I believe so."

"You believe so?"

"Yes."

"But you're not sure?"

"Well, from what I've heard lately it may not be, but as far as I know it's my name."

The footage brought smirks from the jurors. They couldn't help themselves. I chose to react with a loud chuckle, hoping Clark would hear me. He knew I was right behind him, he knew my voice, and I wanted to unsettle him. I too was a fairly complicated reader of complicated human situations (when I wished to be), and what I'd learned was that, inside a courtroom, everyone has an effect on everyone else. There are feedback loops within feedback loops, that is, and they spin in all directions. To the jury, I was a journalist with a notepad whose reactions were legally irrelevant but important for that very reason, because I presumably channeled a point of view—the informed opinion of the media—that juries are forbidden to pay attention to but are bound to pick up hints of here and there. To Clark's top-dollar, imported Boston attorneys, who knew that I was not only a reporter but their client's disillusioned former friend, I was a potential shaper of their public reputations because I might choose to praise or criticize them in the article and book I was writing. To Balian, I was a surrogate, outside juror whose behavior might indicate what the actual jurors were thinking about his case. To Clark? I must have been one more demon in the chorus. My feelings toward him would shift from day to day, but on the day of the bones I truly loathed him, indulging a dark capacity in my nature for which I might never have a sounder excuse. Plus I felt safe that day; he was trapped, hemmed in, and I was flanked by allies, my fellow reporters, who shared my mocking disposition.

The clip from the *Today* show wasn't finished. Balian pushed Play and the interview resumed.

"What do you remember about your childhood?" the interviewer asked.

"Well, I remember clearly going to Mount Rushmore in the back of a woody wagon. And being, uh, uh, an aficionado of station wagons, I, uh, believe it was a '68 Ford. With the, uh, flip-up headlights."

"So you have a clear memory of this car—"

"I have that—"

"—But nothing else?"

"I have a clear memory of once picking strawberries in Oregon."

I restrained myself this time, no chuckle necessary. As the TV Clark dug deeper into his pile of half-formed, bogus recollections ("There are certain things that I haven't forgotten. For example, the garbage strike in New York, I remember that very clearly"), the courtroom Clark visibly labored to dematerialize. What could be harder for a first-rate thespian than to watch himself performing old, fourth-rate bits while being observed in the round, from every angle, by an audience made up entirely of critics? But that was the thing: he wasn't a first-rate thespian, not on TV and not in life, because I could remember his past performances, subtracting from them my then–cooperative spirit. For instance, the time he told me at the Lotos Club that his sister was locked up in a mental hospital, which he said was proof of his family's callousness. The problem was that he'd told me not long before that he had no family: his parents had perished in a car wreck while driving up to visit him at Yale, he said, and he had no other siblings. "What family do you mean?" I should have asked him, and I recall wanting to do so. But I didn't. A spry old waiter had just delivered our drinks as well as a fresh bowl of nuts—why spoil the moment? (Years later, as though he'd filed away his statements and noted a future need to clarify them, he'd say that his "family" was an aunt and uncle.)

It wasn't Clark's acting that dazzled, I realized now, it was his directing, his use of props, and his reliance on atmospheric assistance. On the *Today* show broadcast, though, away from his sets and casts of extras, with no one to help him but a bearded old lawyer, later fired, who seemed both complacent and annoyed, arch little Clark, the pretentious semiamnesiac, was purely summer stock.

"Did you kill John and Linda Sohus?"

"My entire life," he said, his voice like a figgy pudding or an aged cheese, "I've always been a pacifist. I'm a Quaker and, uh, I believe in nonviolence. And, uh, I can fairly certainly say that I've never hurt anyone, physically."

Balian quite wisely left it there, no commentary, no telegraphic gestures, nothing but silence and a screen gone blank and memories of a fudgy, moldy accent. I wished the trial itself could end there too, with the damning, supercilious echo of a man declaring his innocence not directly, with a plain denial, but with a roundabout, syllogistic utterance meant to prove him incapable of violence because he belonged to a sect that preaches gentleness. A full confession could not have been more damaging. Did the jurors appreciate what they had just seen?

Their expressions were intentionally hard to read; they

were taking their work more seriously now. For confirmation of my sense that Balian had put Clark in a tight spot, I nudged Girardot next to me, whose fingers were spider-legging across his keyboard. He nodded, well aware of what I wanted; we'd become friends, and he knew the case in detail, having been there when the body was exhumed, but he was reluctant to compromise his dignity by granting me the showy wink I craved. He believed the defendant was guilty too ("Guilty as shit," he'd told me one day at lunch when we were trading theories about the crime), but he didn't long to see him horsewhipped the way that I was starting to. Like Linda Deutsch, the ace legal reporter from the AP, whose career dated back to the Charles Manson trial, Girardot predicted that Clark would be acquitted. I took their word for this, but their seeming detachment about the prospect was impossible for me to share. They didn't fear him knocking at their door one day, "Long time, no speak."

BRAD BAILEY, WHO'D FLOWN in from Boston with his partner, the white-haired, patrician-looking Jeffrey Denner, opened Clark's defense. Handsome, tall, and formidably gesticulative, with a flap of brown hair that swung across his eyes whenever he grew animated, he was a man of imposing physicality who liked to wave his glasses in the air, jut out his chin, and arch his full, dark eyebrows. While Balian's appeal was to the head, to the faculty of reason, Bailey aimed at a lower, emotional center, at the meeting point of the libido and the gut. Big bones shifted under his suit as he stood up and loomingly approached the jury box. "You tell me," he said to Judge Lomeli, "if I'm invading the province of the jury at any point." He wasn't genuinely seeking boundaries; he was indicating his aim to cross them.

His opening statement was light on substance but packed with rhyme and syncopation. Johnnie Cochran's singsong line from the O. J. Simpson trial—"If the glove doesn't fit, you must acquit"—seemed to be his inspirational text. It appeared he'd decided that LA juries were as childish as the cynics claimed.

"Now, over the next few weeks you're going to learn a lot about a case that is, as you already know, quite old—twenty-eight years—was once quite cold (I submit the evidence will show for twenty-six years), but which still involves a story that is still untold. And as you listen to the evidence in this case unfold, I want you to think about that phrase: 'Quite old, once cold, story still untold.'"

The verse was impossible not to think about, since Bailey repeated it every few minutes, a Beat poet–hypnotist costumed as a lawyer. Between recitations, he heaped derision on the charges against his client, dismissing the murder investigation as "an unidentified bones-in-a-bag case" and "a case about some bones, unidentified human bones in some plastic bags." This naked attempt to depersonalize the victim, to reduce him to a fossil, struck me as both risky and repulsive, but Bailey persisted with the tactic. "And you'll hear, as the evidence unfolds, there was a little bit of difficulty in identifying them [the bones] because Mr. Sohus was adopted, and because a large portion of them were inadvertently cremated."

Having reduced John Sohus to debris—perplexing, adopted, incinerated debris—Bailey shifted his focus to the defendant, whom he sought to humanize. As Clark sat up straight, exhibiting himself, a stage magician assuring an audience that there was nothing up his sleeves, Bailey listed his client's assumed identities, casting them as silly, harmless stage names. They didn't prove Clark was a killer on the run, they showed him to be a snaky flim-flam artist plying an age-old California racket. "As if our client were the first person in this city to try to reinvent himself," he said. This pretty good zinger scored him his first point. Some jurors' heads bobbed.

His next move, which he performed in the grand manner, with lots of admonitory finger-wagging and melodramatic vocal swoops, was to incriminate the missing woman. Everyone close to the trial knew this was coming, including Ellen Sohus, John Sohus's sister, an angular, sleekly dressed Tucson psychotherapist who sat across from me in a cordoned-off section that allowed her to mourn and meditate unmolested. Before she vanished, Linda had acted oddly, telling friends that she and John had been recruited by persons unknown for some kind of confidential government mission that would take them to the East Coast. The mission would call on John's computer background and also on her art training, she'd said, though how painting centaurs and fairies in rainbow colors could aid the cause of national security went unexplained, and apparently no one asked her. Whether she found the tale credible herself was also impossible to know; she may have been forced to recite it from a script.

"And we will ask you," Bailey said, "as you hear this evidence, to start considering whether this might have been part of a premeditated, prearranged way for her, Linda Sohus, to start covering her own tracks, a way for her to confuse her friends, or to set up a getaway, or create a smoke screen for after she had murdered her husband, as she may have been planning for whatever reason, for whatever motive she might have had."

My own preliminary theory concerning Linda's strange behavior, which I'd tried out on Girardot, was that Clark had killed John first and used his disappearance—or even his corpse—to make Linda fear that she too was in peril and needed to throw the assassins off her trail. With another defendant this notion might seem far-fetched, but I knew from experience about Clark's gift for spinning seductive, conspiratorial yarns. There was also a chance he'd told Linda that he himself was a target of the evildoers. Either way, the talk of secret missions originated with him, I had no doubt. Clark's narrative DNA was unmistakable.

Bailey, rising to operatic levels of assonance and alliteration, proceeded to tag Linda with all the traits—duplicity, fabulism, cunning—belonging to the man who'd likely murdered her. He accused her of practicing "the three Ds of Detach, Divert, and Disappear," which I hadn't known until then comprised a trio. He maintained that "as what's untold begins to unfold in this case that's old and was once quite cold," the jury would learn that Linda too had at times employed an alias, "Cody" (the name with which she'd signed her unicorn paintings). How she differed physically from Clark was also deemed incriminating. While he weighed a mere 140 pounds and stood a skimpy five foot six, she was a 200-pound six-footer whose stout Amazonian frame was built to order, Bailey implied, for such taxing labors as bludgeoning and grave digging.

Clark looked smugly pleased with Bailey's statement, and especially with its flattering conclusion. With mind-snapping, topsy-turvy logic, Bailey argued that his "conman" client was simply too "smart" and "crafty" to wrap the skull in "not just one bag, but two bags" of a kind that would flatly link him to the crime. To leave such a "calling card" would be beneath him. The underlying conclusion was clear: the very fact that this murder had been solved (forget the freakish twists of fate involved, from the kidnapping to the swimming-pool excavation; and forget that Linda's fate remained an enigma) demonstrated that Clark had not committed it. He was too brilliant, too slippery, too shrewd. He was the type that *got away* with murder, not the type that got charged with it. If Clark had slain John Sohus, we wouldn't be here, and Clark most certainly wouldn't be here. Yet here he was. There must be some mistake.

SIX

BALIAN WOULD CALL two sorts of witnesses during the trial: specialists and laymen. The specialists would address the case in narrow terms, according to their expertise and training. They would speak about bloodstains in the guesthouse, the physiology of the fractured skull, the faded logos on the bookstore bags, and the timeline of the defendant's movements after he left California in the truck and began his new life of escalating impostures on the East Coast. What they couldn't illuminate, however, was the fathomless human genius for credulity, wishful thinking, and self-deception that had allowed

Clark very nearly to get away with murder, and with so much else. This was the job of his friends, employers, and lovers. I saw parts of myself in nearly all of them, and each time I did I felt angrier and sadder, if a bit less lonesome. We were the fools who were never supposed to meet, the very opposite of a conspiracy, who'd worked together for his betterment, oblivious and separate.

"Never once in all your relationship did he, this allegedly wealthy guy, ever pick up a check," said Bailey, cross-examining one of the first witnesses. "From what you could see, right?"

"He bought me a doughnut after we saw *Double Indemnity*," the witness, Dana Farrar, replied.

Now a special education teacher, Farrar had studied journalism at USC and knew Clark in his guise as a footloose baronet. He told her he'd been raised in South Africa. She ran across him on campus now and then with scripts from the film library tucked under his arm. She assumed he was a student. She once let him lead her through some bushes to crash a party hosted by George Lucas.

On a spring evening in 1985, a few months after the murder, Clark had invited her to join him and some others in a game of Trivial Pursuit. Farrar participated, though she believed that Clark was, in the words of her father, "as full of shit as a Christmas goose." Tables were set up in the backyard between the guesthouse and the main house, which Clark entered several times during the party to fetch glasses, spoons, and sugar for the iced tea he served. He said his landlord was gone and wouldn't mind. At some point during the game, Farrar looked over to her right and spotted what she described in court as as a "rectangle" or "strip" of "crumbled dirt" measuring "two or three feet wide by about five to eight feet long."

She asked her host about the disturbed earth and he told her it was the work of plumbers.

Farrar thought no more about the game night until 1994, when her husband saw a photo of Clark, or Chichester, on an episode of *Unsolved Mysteries* devoted to the Sohus case. John's buried skeleton had just been found, and Robert Culp, the show's host, was asking viewers for information about the missing boarder. Farrar called the police. How they handled her call, or any others they may have fielded after the program aired, is itself an unsolved mystery.

Bailey, a former prosecutor, attacked her credibility scattershot, an approach he would use throughout the trial, particularly with female witnesses. His questions were long and framed as skeptical summaries of Farrar's previous statements to the authorities. He implied that her willingness to humor Clark in his seemingly preposterous claims about his noble pedigree stemmed from some base, ulterior motive—a desire for prestige by proximity, perhaps. He insinuated that she'd called the cops not to aid the cause of justice but to seek attention, to feel important. He hinted that her involvement in the case arose from her unfulfilled career ambitions as a journalist.

He accused her, that is—without coming out and saying

it—of being a certain kind of woman: conceited, disingen-
uous, and dissatisfied. The universal misogynist caricature.

I'd never gone in for academic gender theories, but Bailey's
cross-examination strategy—with Farrar and other women
to come—convinced me that the culture of criminal justice
has a fundamentally masculine tilt. Repeatedly, in a manner that I suspected was typical in modern courtrooms, he
portrayed the female mind as intrinsically unreliable, ruled
by emotion, immune to logic, prone to pettiness, swayed by
lust, and corrupted by vanity. It rarely spoke plainly. It was
seldom candid. It was composed of layers of hidden agendas.
It put up a front, behind which was another front. It either
aimed to please or to conceal, which were often the same
thing. The only way to get the truth from it was to push and
prod until it snapped. Make it angry. Make it cry.

Farrar got angry. Steely, rather. A gate came down over
her face. A short-haired woman with a confident bearing,
she squared her shoulders, set her sturdy jaw, and deflected
sally after sally from her needling, patronizing interroga-
tor. Clark sat up extra straight to back his man. The words
exchanged hardly mattered by this point; the match was
chemical and primal. It was also subliminally symbolic. In
his opening statement, Bailey had asked the jurors to close
their eyes and imagine Linda Sohus—like Farrar, a solid
specimen—striking her diminutive husband dead. A live
display of flashing female ire might help them perform this
desired mental exercise.

"Do you recall telling folks at the *Los Angeles Times*, when you saw this photograph of him, 'That's him, I know those beady eyes?'"

"That might have happened," said Farrar, visibly suppressing her indignation at Bailey's implied portrayal of her as a wicked busybody.

"It doesn't sound very friendly, does it?"

"Well, this wasn't the person I thought I knew, was it?"

"I have nothing further," Bailey said.

He'd failed to drive home what seemed to be his point, that something about Clark provoked hysteria in a certain type of woman, and maybe this partly accounted for his being here, the victim of a witchy warlock hunt. Maybe next time. The witness was excused. It didn't help the defense that a San Marino police officer who'd gotten up before Farrar described, in testimony that was later struck as hearsay, a report from a neighbor of the Sohus's about Chichester burying something in the backyard.

I SUPPOSE THAT IF you can cut a man in three and store his remains in plastic for a time while devising some way to dispose of them more permanently, you can also drink iced tea and play a companionable board game near his grave. Though why would you want to? Dostoyevsky might know. Some guilty urge to confess without confessing or some arrogant urge to bring others to the scene and exult in their blindness to its meaning? Maybe Clark was testing his own nerve that day. If he could calmly answer trivia questions about old TV shows while sitting near a corpse, in range of the beating of its telltale heart, then nothing would ever rattle him again.

The problem of the Trivial Pursuit game, however, wasn't as baffling as it seemed. It wasn't even a psychological matter. It was literary, cinematic. I knew from several sources that my old friend was a fanatical lover of film noir (as Farrar's doughnut remark had just confirmed) and a fan of Hitchcock in particular. He'd surely seen *Rope*, Hitchcock's 1948 Technicolor reworking of the case of Leopold and Loeb, the wealthy young self-described Nietzschean "supermen" who sought to demonstrate their superior intellects by kidnapping and killing a Chicago boy in 1924. The card party was a straightforward homage to the movie's protracted central scene.

I watched *Rope* that night on my computer while sitting on my deck in Malibu with heavy surf shaking the pilings of the building. The movie was the second selection of what I would later come to call the 2013 Clark Rockefeller Film Festival, a four-week event that finally taught me more about the defendant's thinking than I was able to learn inside the courtroom. The first film I watched was Hitchcock's version of Patricia Highsmith's 1950 novel, *Strangers on a Train*. It involved that anachronistic theme, a common one in the middle of the last century, before the culture's hallmark homicides became mass slaughters by firearms in public places, of the "perfect murder." Robert Walker plays Bruno, the mother-smothered creep, unctuous and sexually ambiguous in a manner not dissimilar to Clark, who throttles an acquaintance's hated wife. The plot is an elegant contrivance, but what grabbed me was Walker's sticky portrayal of the wheedling character, who was closer to Clark in affect and comportment than anyone I'd ever met in life.

Rope was a different story, with direct dramatic parallels to the Sohus murder. Brandon and Phillip, the killers, are friends from prep school who live together in a fine New York apartment glittering with crystal and antiques and blessed with a view of rooftops and office towers worthy of the Sky Club. They strangle a former classmate, David (an "inferior being" and the "perfect victim") and stash his body in a wooden chest. Brandon sets two candelabras on the chest in preparation for a social evening that will include the victim's fiancée and the headmaster of the boys' old school (played by Jimmy Stewart) who introduced them to German nihilism.

"I always wished for more artistic talent," Brandon, the sociopathic dandy, reflects before the gathering. "Well, murder can be an art too. The power to kill can be just as satisfying as the power to create." Phillip is less brave, and wonders aloud if they ought to cancel the party. Brandon will have none of it. "The party," he says, "is the inspired finishing touch to our work. It's the signature of the artist. Not to have it would be like painting a picture and not hanging it."

Part Agatha Christie novel, part Noel Coward play, *Rope* confines itself to a single evening of uneasy, ironic, corpse-side chitchat. Brandon delights in the tension, but Phillip hates it, particularly after his old teacher reveals to the guests that he, Phillip, once amused himself by wringing the necks of live chickens. This detail froze me. At lunch with Girardot a few days earlier, I'd learned about a sex scandal dating back to the early 1980s and centered at the Episcopal church, St. James, where Clark first entered Pasadena society and befriended the priest. Girardot had covered the story for his paper, but suppressed its most horrifying aspect: the decapitation of poultry inside the church. As men from the church's inner circle performed sex acts with immigrant laborers, they sprinkled themselves in fresh chicken blood. There was no proof that Clark played any role in this, but Girardot had his suspicions.

I finished watching *Rope*, got on the Internet, and researched the Leopold and Loeb case. Through the sliding glass doors of my apartment the moon-silvered ocean reared up in waves that broke across the sand and slid back down in sheets and lines of foam. I read that Loeb, the crime's instigator and mastermind, had actually enrolled at the University of Chicago at the same age that Clark had told me he'd entered Yale: fourteen. He'd been tutored by nannies until then— another chiller. To aid in a potential getaway, Loeb and his partner spent months before the murder checking into hotels under false names and establishing alternate identities.

The murder, a crime of consummate dispassion (it gave us the term "thrill kill"), occurred on May 21, 1924. The fourteen-year-old victim was chosen at random, as he was walking home from school. The killers lured him into their rented car and attacked him from behind, driving a chisel into his skull. When he failed to succumb immediately, his assailants jammed a sock down his throat. They drove through Chicago in their bloody car until they reached a swamp they'd scouted earlier. They poured acid on the body and then pushed it into a culvert. When they got home they wound down by playing cards.

In court, when asked to estimate the date of the graveside Trivial Pursuit game, Farrar had answered: "Well, USC finished in early to mid–May, and I left on June 13 [for Europe], so sometime in there."

Perhaps Clark's homage to the dinner party in *Rope* was also a kind of anniversary party.

The lucky break that led to the solution of the Leopold and Loeb case was almost as unlikely as the chance unearthing of John Sohus's plastic-wrapped remains. While hiding the victim's body in the swamp, Leopold dropped his glasses. Only three pairs had ever been sold in the Chicago area. He told police he'd lost them during a birdwatching trip. Then he broke down and confessed, as did his partner. To save their beloved sons from hanging, the killers' families hired Clarence Darrow, the era's crusading voice of reason with the famously unruly hair that he was always sweeping back out of his eyes as though to convey the importance of seeing things clearly. His twelve-hour closing statement in the case was an eclectic oratorical opus that drew on philosophy, poetry, and psychology to argue that human beings are pawns of fate, their actions determined by forces beyond their wills.

"Nature is strong and she is pitiless. She works in her own mysterious ways," said Darrow, "and we are her victims. We have not much to do with it ourselves. Nature takes this job in hand, and we play our parts."

The state's attorney, Robert Crowe, preached an older, homelier theology:

"I think that when the glasses Leopold had not worn for three months, glasses that he no longer needed, dropped from his pocket at night, the hand of God was at work in this case. He may not have believed in a God, but if he has listened and paid attention and thought as the evidence was unfolded, he must begin to believe there is a God now."

Darrow's eloquence spared the killers the gallows and led, experts say, to the gradual decline of capital punishment for murder. Since Clark, if convicted, faced life in prison at worst for a crime that might once have earned him death, Darrow was in a sense his benefactor. But if Clark understood this—perhaps as a result of reading up on Leopold and Loeb—I doubt that he harbored any gratitude. I doubt that Darrow's enlightened liberalism meant any more to him than Crowe's Old Testament God. Nietzsche's *Übermensch*, however, would hold appeal for him. "Aren't people stupid," I recalled him often saying, and shamefully I recalled myself agreeing, though the pretexts for his comment now escaped me. A thread of contempt was woven through our friendship, shared contempt for all who weren't quite . . . *Us*. How could one dine at the Sky Club and not feel it?

The building rumbled, half at sea. The moon shone full and dominant, streaming out fine, excitatory white particles that always keep me from sleeping on such nights. My thoughts, of a kind I wasn't used to yet—visual, stacked, out of sequence, ungrammatical—formed a dark slurry as I lay in bed. Movies, even cynical, vicious movies, had always been a comfort zone for me. They imposed and secured certain boundaries on reality. As I perceived the matter, the images weren't playing on the screen but moving slightly behind it, just in back of it, and the screen was indeed a screen, protective, solid. It had lost its integrity now. I didn't trust it. Not all that many months ago, on assignment for the *New Republic*, I'd stood near a cordoned-off movie theater parking lot in Aurora, Colorado, the day after a young madman named James Holmes had celebrated the opening night of that summer's Batman movie by dressing as The Joker and gunning down scores of people in the audience. In the parking lot I could still see the victims' blood. The sight was sickening, but I was ready for it; a massacre had occurred here, after all, and that meant gore. What I wasn't prepared to see, and they were everywhere, were all the trampled paper buckets and trails of popcorn.

SEVEN

O THER THAN ELMER and Jean Kelln, the old
California dentist and his wife who had picked
Clark up on that rainy German roadside and
were surprised to receive his call soon afterward informing
them that he was in Connecticut working as "a ski instruc-
tor," Edward Savio was the only witness who'd known the
defendant in his original form, before he started reprogram-
ming himself. It was Savio's parents who took in Christian
Gerhartsreiter as a foreign exchange student in Berlin, Connecticut, a grayer, less fanciful, harder-trudging town than
San Marino, that rosebush on a cake. Their home served as

the research lab, the incubator, for the experimental selves to come.

"Did you notice him changing his personality and the way he acted around different people in different situations?" Balian asked Savio, a handsome novelist and screenwriter in the fantasy–science fiction mode.

"Yes. He would start to tell a story, and if the person didn't respond well, if they kind of went like [Savio mimed exasperation or skepticism], you know, like that might be a little bit of BS or might be too much, he would notice it, he would stop. You would never hear that story again and he would move on."

Having grown up to be an author, or, as he styled himself on the Internet, a "neo-confabulator" (*Battle for Forever* and *Idiots in the Machine* were a couple of his books), Savio was well equipped to describe the defendant's creative process, its mechanisms and themes. It began with careful linguistic modifications: "He tried to affect what I think at the time he thought was an American accent. And he would practice things, each just with me sitting there, like 'Pass me the bread . . .'" There were also adjustments of behavior, customized for the audience at hand. Around jocks, according to Savio, the defendant was "more relaxed." Around people he deemed his social inferiors "and didn't feel were worthy of his time," he would "just be very short" and "wouldn't even affect his speech much."

I felt a sense of recognition, hearing this. The careful edits and revisions practiced by the ambitious German eighteen-year-old as he gentrified and Americanized himself ("We talked about sort of living the American dream," remembered Savio) resembled literary operations that I performed daily at my desk. The difference was that my artistic guesswork occurred in isolation, while Clark got to test his drafts and sketches in front of a living, responsive audience. I imagined the satisfaction he must have felt when one of his tales or invented manners hit home, drawing a smile or a nod, causing a face to soften and turn receptive. I had to wait months or years for the equivalents of such communicative rewards, and when they came—if they ever came at all—it was in the disembodied form of letters, e-mails, and reviews. There was much to envy in his approach. He didn't live by writing, he wrote by living.

That's how I'd started, too, come to think of it. With poses.

In 1975, when I was twelve, my family packed a U-Haul van, snapped a Yale padlock on its rear loading door, and left predictable rural Minnesota for burgeoning, anarchic Phoenix. My father longed to enter private practice after years at 3M, the company that made Post-it notes, Scotch Tape, and a panoply of humdrum widgets suited to the Office Age. Having always fancied himself a maverick, too large of soul for petty corporate politics, he pined for the sagebrush swagger of the West. He bought a four-wheel-drive Ford Bronco, cowboy boots, and a leather vest, grew a mustache, started lifting weights, and reinvented himself as a tough hombre. My mother didn't change; she was still a nurse.

She dressed conservatively around the house and put on her whites when she left for the ER.

I made some alterations of my own, more out of social necessity than choice. My huge and befuddling new middle school located next to Central Avenue, the city's filthy, felonious main drag, was rife with impenetrable in-groups. Some of the cliques amounted to junior gangs. There were Latino gangs, black gangs, white gangs, and two native gangs, one Navajo, one Hopi. After my first invisible month among them, I started juicing up my past. I told some Mexican girls with cigarette breath and precociously mascaraed lashes that I'd served time in a juvenile detention camp for stealing a chain saw and cutting down some power poles. I also told several stories about a bloodhound that I'd supposedly owned in Minnesota. It had tracked down a lost little deaf girl and saved her life. It had also saved my life by dragging me from a car wreck. I offered a large scar on my right knee and a smaller one on my right hand as evidence of this awful accident. (The knee scar came from falling off my bike, the hand scar from fumbling a knife while carving a pumpkin.) I named the dog Sherlock and told people he drowned during a fishing trip on Lake Superior, when a storm came up and swamped our boat, and Sherlock, instead of swimming for the shore, paddled off into oblivion chasing my floating Minnesota Twins cap. My sense was that half the kids I told believed me and those who didn't either didn't care or appreciated hearing my crap because it meant I would have to listen to theirs.

My father's law practice tanked within a year, a casualty of crackpot clients seeking patents for mileage-boosting magnets and spider venom–based arthritis salves. We ended up back where we'd started, in Minnesota, but farther out in the country than before. Some kids at the school had little reason to be there; they were farm kids, and farming was all they'd ever do. Others were sons of plumbers and backhoe operators, already apprenticed to their fathers' trades. I downplayed my collegiate ambitions to blend in with them, feigning enthusiasm for cars and sports and faking crushes on the popular girls, those devious semen stealers whose secret wish, I feared, was to be pregnant and married by nineteen, all snug in a trailer on their parents' land. Then came the breakaway moment, the SAT exam, which I did well on; its verbal section seemed designed for a loquacious opportunist like me. My scores brought an offer of early admission to Macalester College in Saint Paul. I grabbed my chance. Once there, I stopped suppressing certain interests of mine such as writing poetry and picked up some new ones—punk rock, hallucinogens—sometimes from classmates I found especially impressive.

My posing grew more serious when I transferred to Princeton. It was my father's old school, but it was also the City on a Hill for a Minnesota kid with literary tendencies who'd read F. Scott Fitzgerald. When the cab from the airport dropped me at the gate and I beheld the oxidized green tigers guarding the worn stone steps of Nassau Hall, a building that briefly housed the nation's capital back when the nation was governed by a men's club small enough to gather on its steps, I knew that rebellion and artsy nonconformity were my only viable social paths. Acceptance by Princeton's golden elites—the kids who knew "The Vineyard" from "The Cape" and understood in some thoughtless, genetic way that the best clothes are those that disintegrate with character, not the ones that forever look brand new—would require a full-scale brown-nosing campaign that I didn't feel equipped for. My resentments would show; I'd give myself away. No, I would have to break in from the outside.

"Being myself" at Princeton involved some guesswork, but eventually I settled on a persona. I bought a black thrift-store raincoat and wore it everywhere, rarely taking my hands out my pockets except when I had a chance to startle someone by whipping out my silver Zippo and lighting his cigarette with its oily flame. I wrote and helped direct a trio of imitation Beckett plays whose characters stood at strange angles to one another as they spoke their stiff, emphatic lines, which weren't to be confused with natural speech because there is no such thing as natural speech, not in the theater and certainly not in life, the most artificial form of theater because it denies being theater at all. These were maxims I took from books by Frenchmen. The duty of the artist, I read somewhere, probably while I was smoking hash, which is when books about the artist's duty most appealed to me, is to show that artifice is all. That's why I wore my raincoat on clear days. That's why I ate Hershey bars for breakfast, dipping them in tea. That's why I told my actors to face the EXIT signs when they said, "I love you" to each other before walking off in opposite directions. That's why I wasn't surprised when certain classmates from rich New York families and stern New England prep schools began to nod and smile at me at parties, sometimes even slipping off to talk to me once their real friends were too drunk to notice. I was approachable for an angry loner. As the approaches grew more frequent, I wasn't even that angry anymore; the ugly raincoat just made it seem that way. The fact was that I yearned to ditch the thing—it bored me— but by then it was part of my brooding-playwright image, which was bringing me success with girls, especially the girls that I liked best: rich ones who'd spent years in therapy and treated sex as naked theater.

In time I would graduate from Princeton with highest honors, in part because I learned to speak the language of prestigious cultural subversion; the language of paradox, of endless loops, of ever-receding, ever-dissolving everything, of "truth claims" instead of truths, of paradigms lost. I left the place not knowing who I was or what I was or why I ought to care, since selfhood, I'd learned, is nothing more than this: a pronoun ("I"), a verb ("to be"), a tense (the present), and any grammatical sentence that starts this way about which one cares to make a special truth claim:

"I am Walter Kirn."

By the time I left college, I questioned even that one.

Repairing my deconstructed world took years. One thing that helped was writing about my past in the voice of my pre-Princeton self, the Minnesota kid who believed that language belonged to people, not the other way around. I wrote about the farmers I grew up around, old friends at the Mormon church that I'd attended, a beautiful girl who used to cause me problems, my thumbsucking habit, my family, and my dog. I kept it small. I kept it fairly short. I didn't want to spiral off again. I published a book that a critic called faux naive, which I took to mean "intentionally simple" or "innocent on purpose." He seemed dismissive of this approach, almost as though it amounted to dishonesty, but I disagreed, since what could be more honest than trying to recover from insanity?

At thirty, having published two books of fiction and moved out west in a fit of populist yearning, I betrayed myself again. One winter night in Montana, alone and drunk, I noticed a fetching author's photo on the back of a book of short stories in my bathroom. (I'll call her Ellen Moore.) I liked her bow-shaped lips, her taunting eyes. Her stories, about her big New England family and her adventurous sex life in New York, had made her famous. I wrote her a note, reminding her that we'd met once at a party and telling her that I was coming to the city and would like to take her out.

It worked; my boldness won her over. Ten days after arriving in New York I rented a one-room apartment a few blocks from hers so we could see each other more easily. I quit drinking, quit smoking, and tweeded up my wardrobe. Ellen had gone to prep school and college with the Kennedys, John and Caroline, whom we ran into now and then. The encounters dizzied me at first; I'd forgotten how New York can act as a social particle accelerator. John wore a trucker's wallet on his belt, attached with a chain, and startled me with his earnestness; I'd expected him to be a smoothie, not a boyish idealist. Caroline was tough and wry and seemed like a link to some lost era of high adulthood, perhaps that of her parents. She intimidated me. I even met Jackie, with her cartoonish voice and aura of having known everybody worth knowing and tired of all but a few. Being among such people was a kick, but a kick that I got used to. I impressed myself by not dropping their names when I had the chance. Then Ellen broke up with me and instantly turned me from a semi-insider back into a fan, a gawker. There they were, John and Caroline, on television—the one in my mother's living room, where I ate a lot of hot soup after the breakup—attending a formal-dress awards show named after their family and broadcast live from Washington, D.C. There they were on the covers of supermarket magazines back in Montana when I bought pancake syrup.

Ellen's reasons for leaving me were simple: I didn't have enough money or the right friends. She wanted a "bigger" life than I could give her. It crushed me. I'd feared that her circle would close me out someday. In my closet hung a collection of jackets and trousers that I'd bought for our courtship at a swank department store. I emptied their pockets and gave them to Goodwill and resumed my grassroots rebel act, with a vengeance. I'd been to the front and come back wounded; a grenade had blown up in my hand.

———

THE SAVIOS' FOREIGN EXCHANGE student grew insufferable as he fashioned his newly tasteful, well-bred self. He
compared the family, aloud, to "peasants," and he disdained
the mother's simple cooking. This didn't prevent him, of
course, from enjoying their TV. The small screen was giving him big ideas about how fictional snobs behaved. He
was like one of those unconventional pets, a ferret or a pot-
bellied pig, that starts out small and manageable but fattens
with every feeding until it's no longer a pet but an invader,
taking over the whole basement. The family finally tossed
him out of the house. A few years later, in 1983, he again
contacted Edward Savio by phone from California, where
Savio had also moved to pursue the literary career that he
had discussed with Clark when they were in high school
together. Clark told him that he'd become a writer too. It
wasn't true, though perhaps he thought it was, making his
trademark category error: confusing con artistry with actual
artistry, duplicity with creativity. The boast was the last that
Savio heard of him, but if I knew Clark, he kept track somehow of his school friend's germinating career to use as a
model for the development of one of his own speculative
selves. The evidence would show—not just the trial evidence, but outside evidence that would later come to me—
that Clark tended a flourishing secret garden grown from
cloned bits of people he'd gained some knowledge of.

Savio's testimony was much too brief for me; I wanted
more dialogue and longer scenes from Clark's youthful
Frankenstein period in Connecticut. After Savio finished

testifying, yet another former acquaintance of the defendant who'd had to relive decades-old experiences that had perhaps taken effort to live down, I thought of tracking him to the hallway, but my bench inside the courtroom was jam-packed and I was sitting in the middle. I filled in the scenes I wanted from him myself. I pictured a young Clark in my house, snarling about my mother's cuisine. I pictured him hogging our TV and mimicking the voices of fake tycoons to formulate a voice that he'd present as his own a few weeks later. "This lasagna is a tad watery for my palate." He would have been given fifteen minutes, if that, to pack his chinos and deck shoes and grab his passport. The mystery wasn't just whether he'd killed John Sohus, but why no one had murdered him. That he hadn't been was a credit to his host nation. We're a more civilized people than I'd realized for having tolerated such a savage.

EIGHT

O BSERVING THE TRIAL reminded me of church, of those childhood Sundays spent sitting with my family facing our Mormon chapel's holy end, where the sacrament was prepared and God hid out. I wanted Him to come forth and show Himself, a light, a mist, a shimmer, anything, but only when I grew drowsy and shut my eyes did the wished-for materialization seem at hand. At the trial what I longed for as I shifted in my pew, which I wasn't allowed to rise from every few minutes for a refreshing song or pray-along, was a vision of the murder, the crime itself, that everyone up in front kept talking about. Only

Clark could envision it, presumably, and perhaps it was all he envisioned as he sat there, obliged to appear to be thinking of something else. Had John been attacked from behind or from the front, or had the first blow descended from above, while he was in his sleep? From above, I imagined, knowing Clark, who wasn't one to forgo an advantage. But that would mean he killed John in Didi's house, in John and Linda's bedroom, not in Clark's detached apartment out back, where the detectives believed he'd done it. Shutting my eyes didn't help me at the trial. Earthly scenes that inarguably took place but about which you lack essential facts are harder to summon to mind than divine emanations you aren't sure are possible.

The expert witnesses came to help us see. They arrived at the trial equipped with skills and systems and pried at the tabernacle's lid with science, sometimes achieving momentary leverage and freeing a ray or two of negative radiance. You had to look quickly, though, or the dark gleam dissipated. The act itself was hard to bring to life; the tomb, the relics, and the remains were shown repeatedly. These photographs were arresting if slightly confusing because of the circles and arrows drawn all over them, but they made the crime feel ancient, even older than it was, like an event reconstructed by Egyptologists. This allowed Clark to practice his scholarly demeanor, his pose of learned myopia. I found it absurd, as hammy and overplayed as his dithering art-collector act that first day I went to his apartment. Except, I'd bought that act, hadn't I? It only seemed farcical in hindsight. The jury, however, was stuck with now-sight. Worrying.

Forensic investigator Lynn Herrold's specialty was examining and interpreting trace evidence: fibers, plant matter, tire impressions, blood. She was a large woman with a nasal voice and voluminous long gray hair. She took up position in the witness box as though it were her headquarters, her cockpit. The evidence she'd analyzed included the bookstore bags that held the skull, perhaps the most damning exhibits at the trial. She'd used a sophisticated colored light to illuminate the faded print from three decades ago on the University of Wisconsin, Milwaukee bag. The USC bag she read in daylight; as an alumna of the school, she'd had one just like it stored in her garage. She brought her bag into court and held it up. This particular version of the bag ("Trojan Stores, U.S.C.," it read) had only been produced, she testified, from 1979 to 1984.

Herrold had also inspected the button-down shirt that covered John Sohus's severed torso. Deliquescing tissue had soaked the cloth in so much fluid that she could find no blood on it. What interested her were the ruptures in the fabric. Some, she concluded, had been caused by tree or plant roots that penetrated the shirt during its nine years underground. (Roots "like decomposing bodies," she testified, and seek out their "high nitrogen materials.") Other rips and tears, to her trained eye, had been made by a sharp instrument. There were exactly six of these: two on one of the sleeves around the elbow and four on the back of the left shoulder. All six, she said, were the work of the same blade, and some were consistent with defensive wounds.

Herrold had scrutinized the guesthouse too, and removed

a new carpet that had been laid, to search for blood evidence on the concrete floor. Because she found no visible stains, she painted the floor with Luminol, a chemical that reacts with hemoglobin to produce a soft blue glow—"the same reaction in a firefly." Four areas of the floor lit up when treated and were photographed before they faded. The largest blood trace was two feet long and slightly less than two feet wide. The next largest trace was two feet long by one foot. The blood showed what Herrold called a "wiping pattern," the possible result of an attempt to clean up the crime scene with rags or towels.

What disappointed me about Herrold's testimony was its failure to provoke a single discernible shiver in the defendant. In his head was a memory of slaughter and the hectic aftermath of slaughter that must have put lingering pressure on his consciousness. How had he handled living with such imagery? How had he managed to chitchat at the Lotos Club with such abominable scenes inside him? Not that the club was full of psychic triggers for such grisly memories; perhaps that's why he found it such a refuge. (The Safari Club, which I'd passed by on the street in New York and pictured as full of mounted animal heads, would have been another matter.) I had a conjecture about how he'd kept his cool and was keeping it even now. He'd reframed and gentrified the ugly memories, acting them out in upscale contexts contrived to drain them of their horror. He'd met Sandy, for example, at a dress-up game of Clue, the murder-themed board game. The bloody Rothko might have functioned similarly, allowing him to talk about death and gory knife wounds as matters of cultural, not personal, history. Shelby in her faintly gruesome wheelchair might have served his reimagining project too. Maybe nursing poor, battered Shelby had been atonement. I'd seen other animal lovers work that program, smothering their pets with an affection quite unlike the cruelty they showed to people.

Then I remembered something else: in the burial pit the police had found a phone cord tied around the bags that held the head. When Balian first showed its photo in the courtroom I stared at it, thinking it out of place. Now I had a theory. Clark owned a fetish object: the old black telephone that he once described to me as the consummate example of twentieth-century industrial design. Bill Boss, Sandy's father, a retired engineer whom I sometimes sat next to in the courtroom, told a story about a friend of his who'd used a phone of Clark's without permission once. Clark exploded, raging at the man. It occurred to me that the phone might be the murder weapon. (The police never found one.) Its receiver was solid enough to crush a skull—I imagined him clutching the receiver and slamming it down on a head, a globe of bone—and the cord might have served to asphyxiate the victim, which was why Clark had buried it with the body. (There were certainly handier household items with which to secure a bag around a skull.) To keep the phone after the crime, to hold it close, would suit Clark's film noir sensibilities. He might have treated it like the rope in *Rope*, which the killers hid in plain sight during their party.

I also thought back to a scene in another film noir, *Detour*, a cult movie that a cinephile buddy had pressed on me a few months earlier, in which the horrid femme fatale, Anne Savage, is accidentally asphyxiated when she passes out drunk, tangled up in a long phone cord. Anne Savage was a wise-cracking Hollywood bottle blond of a type that obsessed Clark, I'd been told by a woman who knew him in San Marino, went out with him to a noir or two, and once joined him for a game (not outdoors) of Trivial Pursuit, Silver Screen Edition. He "drooled over" Barbara Stanwyck, the woman said, "was hooked on" Gloria Graham, and adored Grace Kelly—the star, I recalled, of *Dial M for Murder.*

A woman named Linda Hausladen followed Herrold. Hausladen was "the licensee manager" for the University of Wisconsin, Milwaukee. Her testimony was brief but devastating. The design of the second book bag that wrapped the skull dated, she said, to a particular three-year period: 1979–82. I looked at Clark, who was writing on his pad almost as though he were taking down the dates. He was playing a role: the independent investigator diligently toiling to crack the case from the unique perspective of the accused. Because he might be suffering from amnesia, there was a chance, in this offbeat script of his, that the clues would lead right back to him. If so, he gave the impression that he'd cooperate in his own punishment. We weren't quite there yet, however. *Be patient, jurors—I'm working as hard to solve this thing as you are.*

I was having his thoughts for him, fed up with having to stare at him and guess them. They came to me in the German accent of a character on *Laugh-In,* the old TV show from the early '70s, played by Henry Gibson. Along with

Werner Klemperer's Colonel Klink from *Hogan's Heroes*, another show of that era, he'd supplied my notion of Nazis as a child, when Nazis and Germans were the same to me. "Very interesting," hissed Gibson, wearing a too-large helmet and rimless glasses and peering out from a leafy hiding place. "Very interesting," went the line, renderered in a thick German accent, "but stupid."

I had Nazis on the brain that day, the result of two movies I'd watched the night before. The first one was a five-minute student film shot in 1984, which I found on the Internet. Called *Suspension*, it was a vile little production set in a gloomy morgue or surgical theater. A lovely young woman lies sleeping on a table dressed in a some sort of institutional smock. Above her face is a blinding ceiling lamp, the kind used in hostile interrogations, and next to her stands a bespectacled young doctor brandishing an oversize syringe. It's him. It's Clark. It's Joseph Mengele. It's a baby-faced angel of ice-cold Aryan death. He turns to fill the syringe from a glass vial and, just as he does, the woman's eyes twitch open. She sees the harsh light. She comprehends her fate. She struggles up off the table, drugged and woozy, and flees down a hallway. Herr Doktor hears her, looks. Cut to her motionless body back on the table. Cut to the ceiling light, distorted, glaring. Blackness then. Darkness. A single blurry credit: "Chris Chichester."

The second movie was less distressing. Orson Welles's *The Stranger*, the director's first venture into noir, was made in 1946 and is thought to be the earliest Hollywood film to incorporate actual footage of concentration camps. Welles plays Franz

Kindler, a fugitive Nazi war criminal posing as a Connecticut prep school teacher named Charles Rankin. One day a former confederate from the fatherland, who is being tracked by an Allied Nazi hunter, Mr. Wilson, played by Edward G. Robinson, shows up to rendezvous with Kindler, who kills his old Reich-mate and buries him in the woods so as to throw Robinson off his trail. When Kindler's girlfriend's pet Irish setter sniffs out the body and starts to dig it up, Kindler slays the dog as well. We don't see this crime, of course (movies, even contemporary graphic ones, shun any representation of such acts; horses may appear to die in battle scenes, but dogs and cats expire offscreen); we just see the creature dead afterward. To catch Kindler, Wilson must convince the girlfriend that Rankin, a seemingly upper-crust American, is really the German mass-murderer—a suspicion borne out at a dinner party one night when Rankin extemporizes about his country of origin as though he's studied the place in depth but never spent much time there himself: "The German sees himself as the innocent victim of world envy and hatred, conspired against, set upon by inferior peoples, inferior nations. He cannot admit to error, much less wrongdoing . . . He still follows his warrior gods, marching to Wagnerian strains, his eyes still fixed upon the fiery sword of Siegfried. And in those subterranean meeting places that you don't believe in, the German's dream world comes alive and he takes his place in shining armor beneath the banner of the Teutonic knights."

———

I ATE LUNCH THAT day with Frank Girardot at Philippe, a downtown culinary landmark with pushed-together long communal tables, sawdust-covered floors, and glass refrigerated cases displaying dishes of Jell-O and rice pudding. For Los Angeles literary pilgrims in search of Raymond Chandler's hard-boiled ghost, Philippe is the spot. Girardot fit in perfectly. He's a Chandleresque character himself, a newshound whose local knowledge is brewed from shoe leather, antacid tablets, day-old doughnuts, and black coffee. In his briefcase he kept a knotted tie that he could throw on to interview high mucky-mucks and whip back off again for street reporting. His car was a black Ford sedan with a huge motor, manufactured chiefly for police use. He'd been at the job since 1984, before which he sold lightbulbs door-to-door. In the courtroom he filed two stories a day and oversaw the Pasadena paper from the laptop balanced on his knees.

"I'm with you on the phone idea," he said. He lifted the bun off his French-dip turkey sandwich and squirted hot mustard on the meat. "I'm with you on the guilty-mind shit too. You know about his Social Security number? The one he used after the murder, in Connecticut?"

I shook my head.

"It belonged to Son of Sam. There's more, though. He had a phony birthday, too: February 29th. It's Richard Ramirez's birthday."

"Who's Ramirez?"

"The Night Stalker. You remember."

I did, but faintly. Girardot clued me in, speaking between

bites and sometimes during them. Ramirez was the Satanic-minded serial killer who terrorized the same area where Clark lived—the San Gabriel Valley—at the same time that Clark became a murderer. Ramirez's specialty was home invasions that ended in sadistic torture sessions, often with gruesome sexual elements followed by ritualistic desecrations of his victims' remains. In one case, he carved out a woman's eyeballs and took them with him in a jewelry box. Another time he used a tube of lipstick to draw a pentagram on a victim's wall. According to Girardot, one of the reasons the Sohus missing-persons case drew less official attention than it might have was the fixation on tracking down Ramirez, whose murder, rape, and mutilation spree—arguably the most baroquely depraved in American history—was reaching its height just then.

"So Clark would have known this was going on?" I said.

"You kidding? The Valley had a werewolf loose."

A werewolf Clark honored by borrowing his birthday. Clark, the blue-blazer and gin-and-tonics man. The Gordon setter fancier. The Yalie. Tony Bennett's next-door neighbor. A Quaker. An Episcopalian too.

We came up with a nickname for him that day at lunch: Hannibal Mitty. It made Girardot laugh. I laughed too, but not from so deep down. Frank was a tough one, a guy who'd seen it all, but he'd never quite seen this one, he admitted. Maybe no one had. Maybe this was new.

Gatsby the Ripper was our second choice.

NINE

HE'D SPECIALIZED IN duping women, though in some cases it was closer to hostage taking and Cold War–era mind control. One after another, in no particular order, they took the stand like agents of vengeful fate in a classical tragedy, incriminating him by bits and pieces. At times during their testimony Clark's third attorney, Danielle Menard, a silent local counsel who asked no questions during the trial, would lean in close to him, whispering and smiling, behaving almost like a girlfriend. With her Chanel bags and her high-heel shoes, she was a glamorous addition to what must have been an extremely expensive defense team that no one could quite figure out how he was paying for. (Denner and Bailey wouldn't discuss the matter.) An attractive blond in her late thirties given to wearing skirts and attention-grabbing low-cut tops, Menard appeared to have a double function: to comfort and calm Clark in moments of distress and to show the jury that he was harmless, someone a woman could huddle with unafraid.

Elaine Siskoff was Clark's first known girlfriend, and she said he was her first boyfriend. She met him as Christopher Gerhart, a fellow student at the University of Wisconsin, Milwaukee in 1980–81. She believed he was from England. Eager to obtain a green card, he asked her to marry him and she refused. He married her sister instead. In January 1982, Siskoff received a card from him postmarked England. The card informed her that he was busy writing and teaching Sunday school to ten-year-olds. She never heard from him again. The card was a ploy; according to immigration records, the defendant never left the country after arriving in 1979. The card bore a sinister similarity to those sent out in the name of Linda Sohus, supposedly from France, after she vanished.

Kathleen Roemer, a neighbor, knew the defendant in San Marino. He ran the Chichester Family Trust, he told her. They attended a concert one night. She didn't like him and didn't want to see him again. He was so full of "crap," she testified, "his eyes were brown." One week she traveled to northern California to house-sit for a relative, leaving urgent instructions with her family not to tell the defendant where she'd gone. A few days later a FedEx package arrived at the house where she was staying. It contained a box of chocolates and a love note. She never found out how he obtained the address. The prosecution used her testimony to demonstrate the defendant's guile and sneakiness. I studied her with an eye toward Clark's taste in women. She was thirty years younger when he'd asked her out, but her on-the-square-side face was probably not all that different now. I compared her to my memory of Sandra, who'd had a rounder face but a similar head-on bearing. I decided Clark went for women of strength, apparent strength. My stereotyping was premature, though; when I saw the woman he'd stayed with longest next to Sandra I erased my mental chalkboard and decided that the exercise was ridiculous given Clark's singularly flexible character.

Mihoko Manabe took the stand during the trial's second week. A slender woman of Japanese descent who seemed pained to be there, she had known the defendant in New York from 1987 to 1994. She fell in love with him, made a life with him, and unwittingly helped him shake the cops after they linked him to the missing couple through the stolen truck. Manabe was the rare witness who didn't get snappy with Clark's attorneys or contextualize away her gullibility. In the trial's long parade of fools, she was the soft-spoken Queen of Sorrows.

Balian made her speak up to tell her story. She'd met the defendant as Christopher Crowe, the notional brother of Cameron Crowe (best known at the time as the writer of *Fast Times at Ridgemont High*) and a self-described former producer of the 1980s revival of the TV series *Alfred Hitch-cock Presents*. She was working in New York as a transla-tor at Nikko Securities, an investment bank, where Crowe was the head of the bond desk, for no clear reason. He had previously worked for the Greenwich, Connecticut, invest-ment firm of SN Phelps, and he went on to work for Kidder Peabody. Bankers seemed to have a weakness for mono-grammed hustlers full of tea and toast; someone would meet Clark at a yacht club and he'd end up running something for the person. The fine young fugitive from California had struck out in show biz, which flaunts its phoniness, but somehow he just couldn't miss on Wall Street.

His hold on Manabe seemed to grow in proportion to the scale of his deceptions. When the management of Nikko fired him after learning that Crowe was not his name, she believed his explanation that he was a British royal in dis-guise. His real name, he told her, was Mountbatten, as in Lord Mountbatten (1900–1979), military hero, uncle of Great Britain's Prince Philip, last Viceroy of India, and as superbly credentialed a nobleman as Crowe could harvest from his encyclopedias. Crowe also told Manabe he had a grandmother, Elizabeth, who lived in Windsor, England. In a manner that must have further flummoxed her, he men-tioned that he hailed from Pasadena, the son of an anesthesi-ologist father and an actress mother. He left her to fill in the blanks as best she could, probably confident that, like most of his targets, she'd give up quickly and take his word for things. Or not take his word and say she did.

One day in 1988, a policeman called Crowe and Manabe's home, asking to speak to him. Crowe convinced Manabe that the lawman was actually a villain plotting to harm him in some dark intrigue. For their own protection, they would have to go underground, he said, and he would have to change his identity. He would now be Clark Rockefeller, a man whose existence she helped render plausible by providing him with a credit card bearing his new name—on her account, of course. When he quit working, she supported him. When he quit driving, she chauffeured him. She broke off relations with her friends and family, helped him dye his hair and eyebrows blond, and accepted his proposal of marriage. Manabe, too, had acquired a new identity. She was the woman who wasn't there.

"And whose idea, was it to walk on opposite sides of the street?" Balian asked.

"It was his idea," Manabe said.

"Whose idea was it never to walk into your building together so no one would know you guys were together?"

"It was his idea," she said quietly.

"I'm sorry?"

"His idea."

"Whose idea was it to stop getting mail at your apartment and start using P.O. boxes?"

"It was his idea."

My pity for the self-effacing witness was largely self-pity, transferred. With Clark, as I knew, it was *always* his idea. One stopped having one's own when in his company. What made this dynamic painful to recall was just how bad his ideas often were. Once, during a phone conversation years before, I mentioned to him that I'd recently started writing for *The Atlantic*. He fell silent, which puzzled me—I would have expected some show of recognition for the name of the country's oldest magazine, a New England institution. I filled him in on *The Atlantic*'s history and said that it had recently changed hands. "I should have bought it myself," Clark said. "Too bad. Perhaps the new owner wants a partner?" He asked me to pass this idea on to my editor, who could send it up the chain. I did so. The publisher wasn't interested.

Manabe's decision to shield her betrothed (who never followed through on his proposal) contorted and constricted her life for years. She agreed to shred their household trash and discard it at remote locations as far away as Pennsylvania. She kept quiet about the phony name he used ("some Jewish name, Abraham or something") when they paid rent to their landlord. She agreed to flee with him to Europe, and didn't question him when he scotched the plan. She accepted his explanation that the passport with his photo in it—a German passport, not a British one—was an artful fake. She cooperated with his demand that she avoid the closet in their apartment where he stored various files and private documents and which he called his "office."

"And when you would try to go in [to the closet], what reactions, if any," asked Balian, "would he have?"

"He would get angry," Manabe said.

It was one of the very few moments in the trial when evidence was presented of Clark's bad temper. It struck me because I couldn't remember an instance of seeing him in an ugly mood. Only after his divorce from Sandy, when he grumbled for most of one winter over the phone about the injustice of the financial settlement and his grievous longing for his lost daughter, did I even discover that he had moods. Even then, though, I envied his composure; after my divorce I'd lost my marbles, sobbing in front of strangers, throwing things, pounding the steering wheel of my car so hard once that I broke a small bone in my right hand. Clark and I drifted apart during those years partly because I sensed that my distress was alien to him, too raw. I avoided his calls, ignored his e-mails, failed to alert him when I traveled east, and didn't let on that I'd been there when I came back. I'd been to New Hampshire a couple of years earlier and stayed the weekend at his strange old mansion—an unsettling visit; I'd blocked it from my mind—but whenever he asked me back, I made excuses, even when he implored. I was crumbling, a wreck; he wouldn't understand. His money and position kept him placid. He lived in a cloud castle. I lived down below. I'd lost my family, my home, and I was broke. Go crying to a Rockefeller. Right.

Manabe escaped him in 1994 when she met someone else, her future husband. She knew by then that her life was not her own and that if she stayed with Clark it never would be. One day she walked out, abandoning their apartment, which originally had been her apartment. He called now and then, once to say he'd moved to Boston, and sometimes he e-mailed her from an address that ended in "Harvard. edu." But he wasn't in Boston; he'd never left New York (he was still in the apartment), and his only link to Harvard was the new woman he'd become involved with, Sandy Boss, who'd graduated from its business school and whom he'd marry the same year—or perhaps had already married when he called. Manabe was free, though; she'd fled the hall of mirrors.

She didn't look once at Clark, nor he at her. When she was excused and walked across the courtroom, she fixed her gaze on the exit. He lowered his. If it was shame he was feeling, or just feigning (the jurors' faces were full of loathing toward him after hearing Manabe, so looking ashamed was the prudent move), he never showed any sign of it again.

"Did you love him?" Balian had asked her.

"Yes, I did."

"Did you believe he loved you?"

"Yes," she said.

THE WEEK THAT MANABE testified, a man named Patrick Rayermann was sworn in. Balian called him not to talk about Clark but to humanize the victim, whom he'd grown up with, counted as a close friend, and portrayed as "warm" and "generous" and "excited about the future of humanity." I was grateful for the change of subject and for the witness's optimistic tone. Rayermann, a blond, blue-eyed retired army colonel who served in the Space and Missile Defense Command, told the court of his days as an Explorer Scout in a post that John Sohus also belonged to. It was attached to Pasadena's Jet Propulsion Laboratory, a branch of Caltech that puts spacecraft into orbit for the U.S. government.

"We discovered early on," said Rayermann, articulating with military precision and drawing from Clark what appeared for all the world to be a look of respect and admiration, "a mutual interest in the future of science and space exploration and science fiction, most notably *Star Trek*. And we used to enjoy, in particular, sharing, trying to stump each other on *Star Trek* trivia. Because we were early Trekkies."

"In a number of ways," Rayermann continued fondly, describing his and John's circle of friends, "we were like the characters currently presented on the TV show *The Big Bang Theory*. You know, we were having a lot of fun together. But other people might be a little surprised as we described or compared theories about the real Big Bang that started the universe, or how we could get to faster-than-light space travel, or maybe actually talking about a current project at JPL that was working to orbit a new satellite or launch a deep-space probe to really bring some of this to reality."

These details thawed a cold spot in my memory, calling me back to a weekend of many years ago that I wasn't eager to revisit. Remembering it in the light of Rayermann's testimony brought up a host of reflections, theories, and questions, one of which I'd long been living with but had never expected to have cleared up, since no one I knew was qualified to address it. This had changed. When Rayermann finished testifying, I followed him out into the hall and asked. I didn't explain the question's origin so as not to prejudice his answer; I posed it as a matter of geopolitics, as an inquiry into the history of espionage.

"Has Communist China, as far as you're aware, ever engaged in kidnapping or killing American space researchers?"

Rayermann, still in solemn witness mode, took the question seriously. He answered it in the negative, definitively, and assured me that his experience in the army put him in a position to know such things. Then he asked me why I'd asked. I told him it was complicated and that there were a number of topics I wanted to discuss with him, beginning with John's and his favorite TV show. Had Chichester ever watched it with them? No. Before today, said Rayermann, he'd never even seen the guy.

I asked him if he was free for dinner.

TEN

I T WAS THE summer of 2002, about a month before
my fortieth birthday and the terrible accident-miracle
involving my son Charlie and the blue truck. Because
I, like the rest of the country, was in a crouch, bracing for
the next bombing, I don't remember the weather that season, just that there was some. I don't remember the headlines, just that they could have been much worse. Clark was
living in New Hampshire, where he'd moved in early 2000
from New York after first retreating to Nantucket following the supposed nervous breakdown that led him to ask
me about staying on my ranch. He'd bought the estate of

the late Judge Learned Hand, a famous mid-century liberal jurist of whom I knew nothing except that I probably should know more. Clark seemed proud of the place and insisted that I come see it every time we spoke.

One reason I finally agreed to visit was that he'd been hounding me for ages about a series of novels he'd written and wanted me to edit, for a fee, which would presumably be more than I'd gotten for hauling Shelby to New York. I was headed to Boston anyway for a meeting with my *Atlantic* editors. I hadn't flown much in the run of months since the World Trade Center fell, and it was time—time to mount up again, to normalize. Still, Clark sniffed out a certain hesitation, and said he'd pulled strings to secure a room for me at his Boston club, the Athenaeum.

The staff treated me like a proper Rockefeller, not the favor-taking guest of one. I hated the establishment nonetheless. Its rooms had an eerie, evacuated quality, as though the club's departed members had inhaled all its air and energy and carried them down into their tombs. Clark loved such lamplit, varnished dessication, but without him beside me fizzing with boasts and tattle I felt out of place. Princeton had had the same effect on me. The density of its traditions weighed on me. I lay in my bedroom with nothing else to do, too jazzed from flying to go to sleep, and meditated on the Yankee heritage that Clark identified with so eagerly. Its New York version stimulated me, exuding glamor and excitement, but its pinched, moralistic New England version unsettled me. I associated it with ghost stories—Shirley

Jackson's *The Haunting of Hill House* and the like—and with Hawthorne's tales of repressed hysteria. The local blend of religion and enlightenment, virtue and reason, left me worse than cold; it struck me as bloodless and inhuman, a formula for manias and crusades. Learned Hand—what a name! Was his portrait around here somewhere? He sounded like a bony, spry old warlock.

At lunch with Robert and Michael, my editors, the talk was of Iraq, the coming war. Michael, who supported it, would later join the troops in Baghdad and be the first U.S. journalist to die there when the Humvee he was riding in was fired on and overturned in a canal. The news would darken my memory of our lunch and throw into high relief its comic element: a long conversation about Clark. Robert had heard my best stories over the years but not my latest one: in the Cornish village barbershop, Clark had sat next to his neighbor, J. D. Salinger, and chatted with him about old movies. This weekend I might even meet the hermit myself. Clark had boned up on his movements through his wife, Colleen, whom he'd met, he said, in village "quilting circles." And how about this one? At some secret, insider auction, Clark had bought Jean-Luc Picard's prop captain's chair from the bridge of the Starship *Enterprise*. He was storing it in a Rhode Island warehouse along with a collection of Buick station wagons—late-model Roadmasters, not antiques—which held an appeal for him that I couldn't fathom. He owned seventeen of these ugly cars, he'd told me, but don't tell Sandy.

My last anecdote, my best, was so far out that reciting it required facial discipline. Since leaving the freelance central banking field, Clark had immersed himself in a research effort aimed at developing futuristic "beyond Speed of Light" propulsion systems for spacecraft. He said the program was backed by the Defense Department and the Boeing corporation, who'd put up the money for a hush-hush company that was performing cutting-edge experiments in a lab based somewhere "across the border." I'd assumed he meant Mexico, which made little sense, since I'd never heard of defense work occurring there. Plausibility hardly mattered in this instance, though; Robert's and Mike's laughter was enough for me. We were all journalists, professional truth-seekers, but one thing we knew about the truth that laymen were prone to disregard was that it need not be literal or factual; the unpredictable human personality was itself a fact.

I set out for New Hampshire after lunch, but traffic and poor directions slowed me down and I reached Cornish toward evening, hours late. Stone walls, white fences, crows on barns—a rich, deciduous, colonial gloom. The town where I grew up in Minnesota, Marine on St. Croix, had been settled by New England merchants whose homes and commercial buildings imitated the clapboard structures I was passing now, but the atmosphere here was nothing like the Midwest. The dust of attics and cellars was in the air. I sensed the presence of wizened bachelor potters working in sheds behind their mothers' houses.

Parked in front of Clark's property, facing the main road, was an empty police car. It looked abandoned. His house was a ponderous old behemoth surrounded by messy heaps of building materials and scarred by what looked like a botched remodeling effort. Whole windows were gone and sheets of siding were missing, exposing filthy structural underlayers. Two columns supported a roof above the porch, but what really seemed to be holding the place together were rodent droppings and spider webs. Behind the building rose towering, aged pine trees whose shadows fell crabbed and arthritic across the lawn. The lawn was expansive and in good, green shape. It offered contrast. It was like a fresh haircut on a drunken tramp.

Clark rushed out to greet me as I parked my rental car—perhaps he'd been watching for me at a window. I hadn't seen him in person in almost two years and he seemed to have lost some polish in the interval; his khakis weren't fresh but country rumpled and in his face were lonesome lines and hollows. No sign of Sandy—he'd said she worked in Boston now, I think, and only came up on weekends. We shook hands, hugged. I sensed his relief at the shedding of his solitude, and his surge of fussy, pent-up sociability made me feel not only welcome but needed, critical. I felt as though I were restarting time for him.

He didn't show me into the house but walked me briskly over the lawn and down a hillside to a shady pond. The pond had a cute name in the manner of eastern country properties, but I forgot it the moment Clark uttered it. His mood changed from gleeful pride to bruised resentment. "The neighbors sneak in through the woods to swim," he said. "I'm always having to run them off. They think they have rights to our pond. It's highly vexing."

"I have the same problem with hunters on my ranch."

"It's trespassing," Clark said. "It's a violation. Certain persons refuse to understand this." His habit of saying "persons" when he meant "people" caught me up short, the way it always did. No one else I knew spoke this way. I didn't get it. Did he think it sounded squire-like, more formal? To me, it sounded tin-eared and legalistic. High-born types sometimes took pains, I'd noticed before, to sound even higher born than they were, like denizens of an aristocratic fairy world, but in my experience it was usually women who did this.

I strolled the grounds with him and absorbed the backlog of all that he'd wanted to say to me, or at least to someone like me, during all the time we'd been apart. (Sometimes I wasn't sure he even knew me; the usual signs of recognition weren't there. He remembered my wife's and children's names and that I was a writer, but not much else.) My impression was that Clark's friendships, if he had any, because he never mentioned any other friends, were narrowly, individually sorted, and the topics defining any two of them didn't overlap. He was, that is, a new person with each one of us, whoever we might be, and what he said to me was not what he said to the others, if they existed. Sometimes I wondered if my problem was liking too many different kinds of people, including types that I didn't like much at all but felt I had something to learn or to gain from.

I'd been there for an hour and he still hadn't invited me inside. We'd reached a stately tree with a ladder leaning against its trunk. Talking, blabbing, he prodded me up the rungs. "See my hive? In the hole there, in the crotch? I've been harvesting wild honey." I peered into the designated declivity, but like other sights with which he'd sought to impress me—the latest being a rare songbird somewhere in a thicket near the pond—the hive was undiscoverable. This was fairly maddening, especially as he continued to effuse about it, characterizing the honey's taste and the personalities of the bees. I strained but saw nothing, then strained harder and saw less. Behind me I felt the pressure of his enthusiasm but I lacked the words to comment on a hive whose shape I could neither see nor clearly picture. "Cool," wouldn't do—he expected more from me, and that simply wasn't how we spoke.

I shut my eyes and tried to summon a picture. I was still trying when he rattled the ladder as a signal that I should climb back down.

The perceptual warping soon intensified. Resuming our tour, he rued the timing of my visit. "Britney Spears was out last week," he said. "You missed her. And it's a shame you can't stay longer. Chancellor Kohl is driving up." I was still trying to integrate the first name into an improvised map of Clark's existence when the second name emerged and rendered the task futile. The effect on me was like what

I had read the best Zen koans produce, suspending or anni-
hilating thought. I drifted free of my own mind. By then,
he'd brought up a new guest, a mathematician, who had
either just stayed there or was scheduled to come, a certain
Dr. Stephen Wolfram.

"Are you familiar with '*cellular automata?*'" he asked me.

"No. Are they his specialty or something?"

He filled me in. It was quite a science lesson. Most of
it sailed right past me, but not the gist: reality was a computer program. The depth and splendor and nuance of the
universe could all be accounted for by the repetition—the
endless, incessant, robotic reiteration—of certain extremely
basic rules or "codes." Information was all and life was an
illusion. Its apparent surprises and swerving, capricious ways
arose from a mathematical effect that Clark, or Wolfram,
called "nonlinearity." Novelty was merely sameness multi-
plied. Mystery was a machine.

Though maybe I'd misunderstood, because I do that,
especially where science is concerned: I make metaphors
of things that aren't and find morals where they don't exist.
In any case, cellular automata delighted Clark because they
accounted for all the mysteries that bedeviled conventional
investigators from various disciplines—cosmologists, biologists, even linguists—and showed all these puzzles to have
the same solution. Reality, as Clark would have me understand it, was on the verge of being figured out, and in a
manner that Einstein, for example, would find shocking.

"Wow, that's cool," I said. My vocabulary was drying up.

"It's an exciting moment," Clark replied.

"You're friends with this Dr. Wolfram? What's he like?"

We were walking so fast that I didn't catch Clark's answer. I'd started to worry that we'd be sleeping outside that night, perhaps in the bee tree, upside down, like bats. He wasn't tiring, he wasn't losing momentum. Maybe he was a cellular automaton whose heart pumped digital blood. We reached a spot on the lawn beside the road that he gestured at significantly but didn't explain the meaning of until we'd gone a few yards farther.

"That's where Shelby died," he said.

I turned my head around, befuddled. I wasn't sure that he'd told me this before. Pretty little Shelby, black and red, withered toward the tail, with those eyes that I thought had said to me, "Save me from being saved," was gone? The dog that I remembered Clark cooing to in his teensy-weensy doggie voice was dead? I cast back over our phone calls but couldn't recall how he'd broken this news to me, which I thought would have left an impression. The curious thing was that I hadn't expected to see her here, suggesting that I was aware of her demise. Life had moved so fast these last few years. All I clearly remembered were the status reports about Shelby's medical progress, how Clark had liberated her from her wheelchair through nutrition and acupuncture and other treatments.

"Someone ran her over with a car," he said. "They didn't stop to inform me. I found her body. It was very sad."

He didn't sound sad reporting how sad he'd been; he

sounded factual. Maybe he'd had to harden himself. Poor Shelby, the plaything of people who wanted the best for her. She'd recovered just enough mobility to meet the fate she'd skirted the first time. My mother had been right: I should have put her down. All I'd done was to place her fate in others' hands until she had figured out how to snatch it back.

Clark finally asked me into the house. The puny front room, which I took to be a station on the way to a more commodious inner room, was where we sat down, on a sofa not new, not nice, but like something frumpy dragged in from an estate sale. I asked about the empty cop car, which I'd misfiled under "Humdrum topics for small talk," not "Jarring sights needing urgent clarification." Clark said, "Oh that." He said "Oh that" a lot, but only during a jailhouse meeting with him after the trial did I grasp the phrase's function. It offered him one and a half seconds to think, which is all that a brain like his requires to summon up a casual-sounding lie.

"A security measure," he said. His explanation was jumbled and incoherent, something to do with China's alleged ambitions to extend its influence into space and technologically leapfrog the United States using any means at its disposal.

Extracting from Clark a context for these remarks would take much of the weekend. The action item heading our formal agenda—my work on his unpublished novels, for a fee—was equally hard to get a fix on. He hadn't divulged the nature of these books to me, and because his actual life was so outlandish, the fictional subjects that might attract him were impossible to guess at. Beside the works of Dr. Stephen Wolfram, his reading tastes were a mystery to me. I'd probed a few times to see if he'd read my books, or even my magazine pieces or reviews, but was always met with a change of subject, or silence. Modesty kept me from pressing the issue, but a time was approaching when our friendship seemed destined to go flat without some reciprocity from his side. We knew no one in common, we shared no deep experiences, and Shelby, who'd brought us together, was in the ground.

At some point as we sat in the bare room I mentioned a small lien on one of my bank accounts for unpaid taxes. "State or federal?" Clark asked me about the tax bill. Federal. He produced a pen and a small notebook he had with him. He tore out a page and wrote a number on it.

"Here," he said. "Call George." As established earlier that evening in a long rant about his people's troubles with the Bush clan, a favorite topic of his, "George" meant the president. The sitting one. My impression was that the clash of dynasties came down to temperamental differences. The Rockefellers were public-spirited, truly devoted to the common good, while the Bushes were out for themselves.

"This isn't the White House switchboard," Clark informed me. "It's his private line. He'll answer personally."

The notebook page was pressed into my palm. Operating on programming, on habit, I thanked him in my best middle-class way for it, but inside I was reeling. The power to call the Commander in Chief at will, though it wasn't a power I ever planned to exercise—the repercussions were inconceivable: a knock on the door from a Secret Service agent?—did not fit neatly into my self-concept. I did, though, glance down at the numerals. There were ten of them. They weren't all sixes, nor did they seem random. They appeared authentic. Compared to what, though? I'd never paused to think about how a presidential phone number might differ from the civilian variety. It wouldn't, I decided. It would be inconspicuous, like this one, in case foreign agents discovered it by accident, perhaps while burglarizing Clark's house. They wouldn't look twice at it. Maybe I shouldn't, either. I wasn't sure I wanted it in my memory, a target for possible interrogations. It couldn't be real. I looked again. It was. An actual phone number, but undialable. There might be consequences.

The scrap of paper was deep inside my pocket when Sandy arrived, an emissary from the normal solar system that was out there somewhere, and which I missed. She looked punished and flayed by adventures in the business world and was wearing those clothes that they make women wear to prove they're serious and don't think of sex much. Words passed between her and Clark about her week but they were few and lacking in warmth, a minimal interaction after an absence. Their sight lines crossed as they spoke but didn't meet; he gazed past her at the door and she gazed past him at a pillow on the sofa. Then Snooks appeared, delivered by a nanny, I think; whoever the person was came

and went in seconds. Clark hogged the child's attention
from the start, instructing her to walk to him. I pretended
to hang on her every step. My stomach gaped. The Rockefeller hosting style, from what little I'd experienced of it,
disdained guests' appetites and physical comfort in favor of
the pleasures of proximity to private family goings-on. I felt
duly privileged, but I needed food.

It never appeared, not that night. Clark, through some
complicated excuse, faded off into the depths of his strange
house to parley with Sandy or attend to Snooks while I
ended up in town, alone, slaking my hunger with convenience food. On my return Clark showed me to my bedroom, which was unfurnished except for a stiff mattress that
I remember as lying on the floor, but which may have sat
on a Spartan, low-slung frame. The thin blankets and pillows starved my soul as I lay down with a book Clark had
provided, a biography of Learned Hand, into which he'd
slipped a piece of paper to mark a passage on "Doveridge,"
the estate. It had been a quite handsome home once—in
a small town or city in the Midwest it might have been a
prestigious mortuary—and Clark's intention was to restore
it to its former glory. For now, though, one suffered here,
and I resented it. The room went from much too warm to
much too cold, and my sleep was turbulent and shallow, an
enervating, semiconscious wrestling match with inner and
outer abusers—bad dreams, spine-deforming low spots in
the mattress. I woke at intervals and read the book. Learned
Hand, what an upright, boring life he'd led.

No one came for me in the morning. No summons to breakfast. I listened hard for indications of bustle or conversation in the house but I didn't feel free to venture farther into it; the unfinished hallway outside my room was dim and forbidding, nothing but dust and echoes. I crept outside, famished, and walked for a good hour along the curving lane where Shelby had died. For a dog owner here not to fence his yard seemed negligent. Clark had hauled in a dummy police car for his own safety but offered "The Shellborg," as he liked to call her during her wheelchair days, no such protection.

For most of the day I entertained myself. Clark was occupied in an office he didn't show me, whose location within the house I couldn't deduce, with a "labor dispute" at his rocket firm, he said. Sandy had gone absent. I made up my mind to leave but didn't do it; there was no one around to say goodbye to. Clark reappeared as the afternoon was ending with a proposal that we eat dinner out and a glancing allusion to Salinger (he "lived across the way") that slightly revived my interest in the visit. I'd promised Mike and Robert down in Boston that if I met the literary legend I'd write about the encounter for *The Atlantic*. The odds of a meeting kept tilting back and forth.

We drove south for about an hour on narrow roads that I remember as passing empty farm stands or handmade signs for farm stands and later on passing lots of rocks and cliffs. Our destination was a café known chiefly for its hot chocolate but that Clark thought we should try out as a dinner spot. As a nondriver, he seemed to relish the trip; he stared out the window like a dreamy kid. I pressed him on kidnap prevention, on Chinese *Lebensraum*.

"Oh that," he said. Then he told me more about Jet Propulsion Physics, his "interstellar travel" engineering firm, which was based, he said, in rural Quebec a couple of hours north of Cornish. The system the firm was working on was based on "the Casimir effect," some force identified by quantum physicists that is created when two particles are placed infinitely close together without actually touching. China had heard the news of this advance. Its space program, a department of its military, had a record of snatching foreign rocket scientists and installing them in its own labs, so why not be cautious? Thus the cop car. Also, Clark said, I should call George Bush tomorrow. I mustn't be shy. It was silly to be shy.

The dinner disappointed. I don't remember what we ate, just a sense of skimpiness and that the menu overpromised. I don't remember what we spoke about; there were so many questions I must have wanted to ask him that I somehow doubt I even tried. The memory that overshadows all else is a small one, but it felt enormous that night: I paid. The meal was on me, and not by choice. It soured me. Clark's no-wallet act was a Wasp standard and seemed beneath him as wizard of quirk. He'd eaten greedily, as though he'd waited, and had maneuvered me into getting dessert after I said I wasn't hungry by ordering dessert himself. I was trying to keep the check down, assuming he'd cover it, and I interpreted his pressure tactic as a command to lighten up and let myself be treated. He'd burned me before. The "stipend." I should have known. But strangely, I thought his mistreatment of me before meant that he'd want to square things now. That's how I would have done it. Weren't we both gentlemen?

The return trip to his crackpot mansion felt tense and endless. The highway ran alongside a wooded river and I repeatedly slowed when taking curves, afraid that I might meet a speeding vehicle that had drifted across the center line. Nothing. We were alone out on the road. Who was this man beside me, anyway? He didn't like or respect me. I shouldn't be here. After our first meeting in New York, after the five-hundred-dollar check, I should have acted as a smart woman does when she's dating someone new and dropped him after one infraction: "See ya." And what was the meaning, anyway, of his excruciating accommodations, the unheated bedroom and the decrepit mattress—was he trying to see how much I'd take from him or, more likely, how little I'd accept?

We drove into Cornish in the gloom that gathers so thickly in barn-and-farm-stand country, the gloom of wher- ever pumpkins are sold roadside and people hang Indian corn on their front doors. Clark's face was turned away, but he seemed conscious of my disenchantment. He brought up Salinger again in an obvious ploy to soften me, saying we'd passed his driveway a mile back or so, but I was finished on that subject. Something had changed between us: me. The summer before I'd published a novel that had been bought by the movies and well reviewed, raising my value in my own eyes. I had two children now. I didn't need friend-ships that felt like hazings. I didn't deserve whippings from on high. We slipped off to bed with rote "Good night"s. I resolved to leave before he got up.

I awoke the next morning to find him in my doorway. We would drive up to Hanover and tour Dartmouth's art museum before it opened for the day ("My aunt built the place; the guard will let us in"), and then, over breakfast, talk about his novels and how I might improve them. "Please," he said. "I've been waiting. I've been patient."

"What are these books of yours even about?"

"I'll tell you once we're there."

"There" meant Dartmouth, which Clark had some con-nection to, making Princeton about the only Ivy League college that he'd neither attended nor hung around for some sort of obscure postgraduate work. Money makes you wel-come everywhere was the lesson I took from this. The cam-pus was austere compared to Princeton's, very New England in its thin, dry aura, and set out in front was a building with ranked white columns whose classicism seemed fake and overbearing. The museum, though, was more modern. Its facade was made of rain- and soot-streaked gray concrete, like the entry to a bunker. Inside was a desk with a guard who Clark approached while I stood back, polite, discreet. The guard, as predicted, unlocked the place for us, which wasn't a guard-like move but sure was Clark-like, in that it pressured someone to betray himself so that Clark could better pass as Clark.

We looked around the permanent collection but not in the reverent, pausing, careful manner of ordinary museum-goers. Clark rammed us along past the paintings he prized most, crisply footnoting what we were seeing and leaving me little time to ponder his comments. I wasn't in an appreciative mood. My mind had no room in it for culture and history. I was plotting my getaway from the situation, my emotional, sentimental exit, not my physical departure. The monologue in the museum was interesting only as a climactic memory of an unbalanced, insulting relationship that had gone on too long and grown disfiguring. The chirping, pedantic, benumbing little prick. I must hate myself at some level; I'd finally acknowledged the obvious. I didn't feel this self-loathing, not that I knew of, but the evidence for it was piled high. He'd needed so little evidence to diagnose me, and I'd needed so much. I felt loathing now, all right, though mostly in the form of loathing for him. It was all very clear just then, my situation, yet still confusing. I should go write something immediately and try to work it out on paper. I resolved to do it.

We sat at a tippy table on the sidewalk and ordered tea and coffee, juice, and pastries. I vowed to myself to make him pay, though maybe it would be better to split the check; dignity lay in holding up one's end of things. Or should I shame him by covering the whole thing? Of course it wouldn't shame him, though it ought to, but maybe beholding further shamelessness would finally force me to act, not merely stew. Tourists went by in their clashing tourist outfits, grumpy with one another, dulled by leisure. I had to get back to work. I couldn't wait. Every moment with Clark was a horrendous waste. I needed an epitaph for him, and it was this: he was a waste and a waster, and on purpose. To think too hard about what his purpose might be would only be a further waste.

"Did you know I consider you my best friend?" he said. It startled me, his perfect timing. I'd been about to throw coffee in his face. "I'll tell you why," he said. You're the only person in my life who doesn't want something from me, who isn't envious. I can't be myself with most persons. It's a curse. With you, though, I'm relaxed and comfortable. I'm grateful for this. What a visit! It's been splendid."

"Thank you," I said. I felt cornered by his effusion. I tore a corner off my pastry and dunked it in my coffee, noticing Clark's expression as I did so. He looked displeased but determined not to show it. I dunked things. He didn't. We came from different worlds. Mine no longer embarrassed me, however, which meant that his was losing power. I felt sure that he sensed this and I was curious about what he'd do to try to gain it back.

He confessed. He invited me deep into his sadness, pinning me under its melancholy flow. His family was atrocious. His uncles and aunts who'd stood in for his dead parents had shooed him along from home to home. His sister, a lunatic, was rotting in some hospital. Unclear to me was whether he missed her or whether her incarceration suited him; I seemed to recall that he'd portrayed her once as something of a burden. He described himself as a wandering, lost soul who had been educated but never nurtured, who had settled for paid-for knowledge as a substitute for priceless affection. The membranes surrounding his light blue eyes turned pink. The wings of his nostrils subtly flared and trembled. People passed by our table with no idea that a Rockefeller was agonizing nearby, pouring out his troubles to a mere Kirn. "America," I remember thinking. "It muddles all of us up together in such strange ways." The melting pot was at full boil.

"Tell me about these novels you've been writing." I asked this, I told myself, to play for time, not because I was truly curious. I managed to stay inwardly remote but my tone was solicitous. If I lured him back into pleasant conversation, I thought, he'd eventually try to dominate it, angering me afresh. I needed fresh anger. He'd sucked it out of me. I needed fresh pain to send me running.

"What?" he said.

"Your books. Your novels. What are they about?"

"Oh, those," he said. "They're homages. They're reworkings. Amusing things to write, but I can't claim they're original."

"Literature's never original," I said. I'd got this idea at Princeton, which had borrowed it from Yale, from Harold Bloom, a professor there. His book was called *The Anxiety of Influence*. It was one of those books whose title tells it all, and that had allowed me to skim it in good conscience.

"My novels are adaptations of memorable episodes from *Star Trek*, the TV series," Clark said.

Star Trek? It helped ground me to speak the words. And

I hoped it disguised my flabbergastedness. "The rights," I said. "Have you obtained the rights? If you want to exploit another trademarked property"—I was channeling my lawyer father's vocabulary, grateful for the cover it provided—"you first have to secure the rights to do so."

"Oh, I'm sure that the person who owns them will sell them to me. You know, Walter, everything is available for a price."

"Right," I said. "That's true." I was still regrouping. I was starting to think the process might take awhile. And maybe I should consider drawing it out. To tease him, and to waste his time for a change. "So each novel, each book, is one . . . ?"

"Episode," he said.

"Interesting." I meant the opposite. I repeated the word to emphasize this fact, in case he'd thought that I was speaking sincerely, not slyly cutting him. "Interesting." It was a word very seldom spoken in earnest when responding to book descriptions, book ideas; but did he know this? It was also a word that if spoken three times turned back into a compliment, I feared. I didn't say it again. I tried to seem far away instead, and drifting further by the millisecond, back to my life, to Montana, beyond his reach. And truly, I was almost there. All I had to do first was give him a ride back home.

"*Star Trek: The Next Generation*," he explained. "You're probably thinking of the original series. Are you? I suspect you are. The original series never grabbed me. I found it terribly inferior. I much preferred the sequel."

ELEVEN

I MET COLONEL RAYERMANN for dinner at the Bona-
ventura Hotel, a spot that he chose for "sentimental reasons." He revealed them to me in the lobby, a
futuristic affair out of the past, soaring, reflective, curved,
and cycloramic—a good place to drink after shrugging off
your space suit following a trip around the galaxy. With
his pilot-like perfect posture, his white, white skin, and
his eyes of milky blue (I'd only seen such eyes on German shepherds), Rayermann looked like he'd done exactly
that: conquered some starry quadrant for our people, been
debriefed, paraded, and returned to base. On his shirt was a

silvery, pointy *Star Trek* emblem that clashed a little with his grown-man's jacket. He also wore a small lapel pin in the form of a spacecraft; a Discus 3, he called it. He was a most specific former soldier, and why he hadn't made general I couldn't imagine. Maybe it was true, what people said about generals: politicians. The colonel wasn't one of those. He lived too close to the facts.

"This is where we crafted the constitution for the Explorer post," he said, referring to the post that he and John belonged to. "December 16, 1971." Then he sipped the cocktail I'd bought for him and that he'd squarely thanked me for. I was ready to buy him another one just to hear again how adroitly the officer class expresses minor gratitude.

Our interview wandered from the start. I was a few years younger than the colonel, but still of an age to groove on matters galactic the way that he and John had in their teens. Since the colonel had had a Top Secret clearance, presumably— the real kind, not the imaginary Clark kind—I asked him first if UFOs existed. He granted me undiscovered alien life forms (a cosmic certainty to his mind) but said he'd spent too long in the army to think that the government could successfully hide a crashed, recovered saucer or a dead Martian. This joke led him down a mournful path as he bemoaned the curtailment of the bold missions that had inspired him in his youth. With the ending of NASA's Shuttle program, America had drawn inward, he believed, and lost some of its spirit of adventure.

When we spoke about his best friend's accused killer,

the colonel ventured an observation that I'd come across once or twice before, in Internet chat room discussions of the case: Clark, the man of many faces, had the skills of a professional spy. "It's almost as though he'd been trained either by the CIA or the KGB," the colonel said. "A few days after he kidnapped his daughter, he had established a completely different identity for himself. Very few people can do that. It takes a very disciplined mind. And a mind that is incredibly capable of compartmentalization. To effectively retire an identity that you've been living under for two months, twenty years, whatever it may be, and immediately slip into being someone else . . ." He shook his head and raised one hand to catch the attention of the cocktail waitress.

"I don't believe he was trained," he said, "but wow . . ." I nodded at him, because I knew the feeling: prolonged proximity to Clark and to the testimony at his trial had opened up a paranoid streak in me. A couple of nights before, on my computer, while sliding around among Web sites doing research on the psychology of murderous narcissists, I'd happened on the ghastly, way-out story of the CIA's MKUL-TRA mind-control project. Revealed to the public in 1975 by a specially appointed panel called, of course, the Rockefeller Commission, this very real and profoundly demented program hatched during the Red Scare 1950s had enlisted countless subjects, some of them witting participants, others not, in a range of Strangelovian experiments involving LSD and other hallucinogens. The goal, it seems, was to counter (or compete with) various "brainwashing" techniques thought to be used by our country's Communist foes— murky Manchurian Candidate–type stuff. The facts of the program were only half the story, though; MKULTRA the myth, the urban legend, was a black octopus of freelance theorizing that choked off rationality in many who studied it. To the self-styled truth-seekers of the midnight Internet, it explained everything, as such theories will, from the assassination of JFK to the formation of the Federal Reserve Bank. According to one fringe Web site I visited, it even explained Clark Rockefeller. He was a zombie of the Power Elite, pharmacologically molded and controlled for purposes malevolent and unfathomable. I spent three minutes on the crackpot site, then shut off my laptop and tried to go to sleep. Impossible. Despite a melatonin capsule followed by a hot bath infused with Epsom salts, my neurons buzzed and sizzled for two more hours.

When dinner arrived, I asked Rayermann about *Star Trek*. He estimated that he and John had seen each episode "approximately" 120 times. He described to me in a way I'd never heard before and that I found strangely poignant under the circumstances the idealistic appeal of the show's ethos, especially for children of the Cold War. "*Star Trek*," he said, "was a very positive vision. No matter what your trials and tribulations are today, there will be a brighter future. We have to work at it, we can't give up, but we will get there. It's about human beings learning to be more equal, in part because we've learned that, wow, there are other intelligent, thinking, space-faring beings in the galaxy."

Rayermann's face grew boyish as he spoke, acquiring a dreamy cast. For the first time since the trial began I could picture John Sohus alive, as something other than a bag of bones or the half-hooded face in a photo of his and Linda's Halloween wedding. John was like Mike, a friend of mine from childhood who had also lived under the spell of science fiction. We read Ray Bradbury paperbacks together. We launched model rockets from a hilltop hay field and ran along under their drifting plastic parachutes until all hope of recovering them was lost. When we were seven, Man landed on the moon—"Man," that long-gone Enlightenment abstraction—and Mike and I stood in the road between our houses and hurled stones straight up into the darkness, trying to hit the flag Armstrong had planted. We were sons of the space race, just like John and Rayermann, enthralled by its expansive, gee-whiz spirit and prone to regard the night sky as a vast prophecy of civilization's potential progress. Around us, in missile silos, jets, and submarines, terrible forces had massed themselves for conflict, but there was also a sense of a broad counterforce pressing onward toward astounding breakthroughs. We might fly someday, personally fly, lofted by jetpacks or one-man helicopters. We might even learn to converse with chimps and dolphins. We might meet a man who'd sailed off past Andromeda and come back younger. We might not have to die. That, or we'd inherit an earth of ashes, our radioactive limbs reduced to stumps. The perils and the promises. The wonder. That sense of intimacy with the infinite could make a boy feel simultaneously tiny and immense.

"What about novels?" I asked Rayermann. "Are there *Star Trek* novels?"

No hesitation. "The first *Star Trek* novel was *Mission to Horatius.*"

"Did John read them?" I asked him.

"Definitely yes."

There, in that space-station lobby with the colonel, who had grown up to do what John had dreamed of doing and Clark had pretended in Cornish he did secretly—and so proficiently the Chinese were stalking him—my theory of psychopathy came together. There was no sign that Clark had been a Trekkie or an aficionado of jet propulsion until he killed a man who was and assumed his fantasies and hobbies. Clark was worse than a murderer and dismemberer and graveside board-game player. He was a cannibal of souls.

He also might be, as Rayermann taught me over dinner, an incarnation of something called "the entity." This term emerged when I challenged his tipsy claim that "everything you need to know, you can learn from *Star Trek.*" All right then, sir: of all the monsters and villains on the series (the original series; the colonel disdained the sequel), were there any resembling the defendant?

The colonel looked off toward the lobby, computing, processing, though not for any longer than ten seconds. "Second season. The crew is on Argelius II, the planet of Love, a place unused to violence. There have been stabbings and killings of several women, and Scotty—Engineer Montgomery Scott—has been found at the scene of one of these crimes. The local authorities put him on trial. It turns out that the culprit is an alien creature, a sort of noncorporeal entity that is more thought and energy than physical and first appeared on earth as Jack the Ripper. When humanity started reaching out to the stars, this creature, this entity, moved with us, preying on other colonies and planets. In the end it's defeated by Kirk and Spock, who set the *Enterprise*'s Transporter beam on 'widest possible dispersion' and blast the entity out into space. The episode—I don't recall its name—ends with a line from McCoy. I think he wonders, 'Can it coalesce again?' "

"The episode is called 'Wolf in the Fold,' " the colonel said. "I would have been pissed at myself if I'd forgotten that."

"It fits."

"*Star Trek* is a remarkable resource, don't you think?"

I granted him this and thanked him for enlightening me, not lightly or facetiously at all but with what I hoped was my own civilian's version of his precision. He'd offered a fact at a moment when facts felt scarce: *Star Trek*—the original, not the sequel—was as helpful a reference work in the present matter as any I'd come across so far. "The entity." It named the restless thing beneath the aliases, the thing that seemed to change but never did. The metaphor might have run away with me if I'd known more about the show that spawned it. Destruction by "widest possible dispersion." That sounded pretty fitting too.

TWELVE

THE DAY THAT Sandra Boss was set to testify, my fourteen-year-old daughter, Maisie, came to court with me; her school in Montana was on a break. I hadn't seen her and her brother in over a month—I was too busy writing and reporting—and we'd spent the weekend, Easter weekend, walking on the beach in Malibu. Dead baby seals had been washing up that spring in what government biologists were calling an "Unusual Mortality Event," and we'd come across five of them that Sunday morning, their bodies evenly spaced along the sand at intervals of fifty yards or so, marked by glittering clouds of circling flies. Some families might have steered clear, but we were fascinated; our years on the ranch had accustomed us to finding carcasses. Deer. Newborn antelope. Badgers. Porcupines. We poked them with sticks and performed impromptu autopsies. "Dad, I love dead things," Maisie had told me once as we stood over the body of a fawn whose throat had been torn by a cougar, or so we guessed. I thought I understood. Death allows a closer study of unfamiliar creatures than life does.

Concerned about looking grown-up in the courtroom, she sat up churchy-proper in a gray cardigan, her waist-length blond hair pushed up into a ball and held with black elastic bands. Her face had my mother's wide Hungarian cheekbones, but her slanted green eyes were an ancestral mystery. She scanned the scene with a look of mastery, the result of the true-crime shows she liked to watch when she came to visit me on weekends. She knew the layout of the room, the protocol, and the roles of all the players down to the implacable stenographer and the bored, portly bailiff with his gun. What she didn't know, though, was that I'd brought her here not just to make a peculiar family memory, but to close a loop with the defendant. Our friendship, when it last felt like a friendship, was, ironically, all about our children, our kindred condition as single, divorced fathers.

The phone calls started in late 2007, just before Christmas, after Clark's split with Sandy. He fumed and moped, resentful and bereft. "She stole her! She stole my darling Snooks!" he moaned. "I have nothing, Walter. There's nothing left." I hadn't heard strong emotion from him before and his overbred voice in despair was an absurdity. His instrument wasn't built to play sad songs. His word of choice, "devastated," pronounced syllabically, made him sound like an Oscar Wilde bachelor mourning something other than a lost daughter—a grease-stained dinner jacket, say, or a cracked champagne flute. He said he was living at his Boston club, and I pictured him lying on a hard divan, his Top-siders kicked off beside him on the rug, in a room full of tea-colored shadows and musty portraits and mean old emaciated wooden furniture. I didn't envy him. Maybe I never had. What I'd wanted, I think, was for him to envy me.

Sometimes he called at night, while I was reading, and I'd leave my book open in front of me while he grumped and growled. I couldn't afford to relapse into bitterness, having survived a long funk of my own. Once he interrupted my kids and me as we were choosing our tokens for a Monopoly game, and for the first time since I'd met him I said I'd call him back later, the next day. I enjoyed this newfound edge; in terms of paternal deprivation, I had a few years of seniority on him. I exploited my rank to advise him on healthy eating and the calming power of regular exercise, but there was no evidence he heard me. In the whole time I'd known him, not one thing that I'd said to him—no story I'd told, no counsel I'd provided, no opinion I'd advanced—had ever come back to me later from his lips.

Whenever I urged Clark to return to court to press for more frequent visits with his daughter, he'd answer that he was broke, wiped out, and that Sandy, by moving with Snooks to England and taking a job at McKinsey's London office, was now beyond his legal reach. His defeatism disheartened me as a father. What did it mean for ordinary men that even someone with his stupendous name and social leverage could be laid so low by laws and lawyers? I feared he'd harm himself. He sounded isolated. Shelby was gone by then. Yates too, I gathered, since he no longer mentioned him.

I touched my daughter's shoulder as Sandra Boss, whose presence had attracted extra press and forced us all to pack in hip to hip, entered the courtroom through its heavy brown doors. Her shoulder-length hair was the blond that covers gray and in her ears were modest single pearls whose luster was that of money banked, not spent. Her bearing was less businesslike than scout-like, and when she raised her truth-affirming right hand, Abe Lincoln sat up straighter in his portrait.

For me, Boss's manner had a touch of overkill. She surely knew there were skeptics in the audience who couldn't square her sterling résumé with her record of gullibility. The Lifetime Channel had aired a movie, *Who Is Clark Rockefeller?*, that had taken her side in the matter of Snooks's abduction but had failed to inquire very deeply into what she was thinking all those years, living with someone who didn't seem to work, never introduced her to his relatives, spent her paychecks, and cruelly derided her mothering.

Like Mihoko Manabe, but in a stronger voice—a posher

voice than I remembered; London had buffed and polished her, it seemed—she told a story of a florid courtship decaying into entrapment and rigidity. Clark was gallant and flattering at first, the only man she'd ever dated, she said, who didn't seem threatened by her intelligence, but soon his obsessions and screwball rules took over. He would always wear some kind of hat when out in public. Whenever they drove together through Connecticut, he forbade her to stop for any reason because his parents' car wreck had occurred there and he considered the state cursed. He refused to set foot in California, another supposedly evil state. He wired the house with ganglia of phone lines associated with different area codes, and even different country codes. He routed the mail to a series of P.O. boxes. Once, she recalled, he let her glimpse a fax—accidentally on purpose, she now felt—whose edge bore the words "Trilateral Commission." When asked if she truly believed that Clark belonged to a group that legions of conspiracy theorists accuse of being a shadow global directorate, her answer, startlingly, was yes. "The idea was that he was a sort of junior member and needed to earn his stripes to advance."

My daughter, after about an hour of this, took my pen and scribbled in my notebook, "It's crazy to think that he's sitting right there with all the answers." This captured it all right. The murder trial of a silent defendant, especially one who has spent a lifetime lying to everyone about almost everything, can't help but strike a child as what it is: a hugely laborious exercise in trying to read a mind. I wondered if he was enjoying this guessing game that he'd lured us into.

Because here we were again, just the way he liked us: tantalized, off-balance, and in the dark. And there he was, protected by his constitutional rights, fixing his wife with a simulated smile that every book on vampires ever written told her not to regard for even an instant.

"What do you think?" I whispered to my daughter as Balian continued with his questions. I was proud of myself for organizing this field trip.

"He seems incredibly lonely," she whispered back.

"That's what happens," I said, "when you never tell the truth."

"I know. Can we be quiet now?"

"The wife's in the mountains somewhere, detectives say. They can't find her body."

"I mean it, Dad. Hush up."

I put my arm around her to further annoy her; I missed her little fits of teenage temper. They reminded me of my power as her father, and also that my power was fading, which was as it ought to be, life's normal course. I almost wished Clark would turn around and see us. I'd succeeded in holding on to what he'd lost, and some boastful part of me wanted him to know it, wanted him to acknowledge that I'd won. It wasn't nice. It was cruel. But men compete.

My daughter took my pad again and wrote, "What's heresay?"

"That's not how it's spelled," I whispered. I spelled it correctly for her.

"What is it, though?" she wrote.

"Something you heard that you repeat. It's not allowed as evidence," I wrote.

"Why not?" she wrote. This was fun. Like junior high.

"It might not be true. It might be a mistake."

She sat and thought a bit, looking from Clark to Balian to Boss and then back at Clark and then down at the pad. "I'm still confused," she whispered. "Hearsay also might be true. What if it is, and it's the only evidence?"

'That would be too bad,' I said.

THE NEWS OF THE kidnapping reached me through the Internet at the end of July 2008. I was in Montana, at my computer preparing to write, a transition that grew harder by the month. Something about the structure of my brain, its associative, porous, open-endedness, was defenseless against the ever-enlarging Web. Every video, news story, photo, e-mail, stock chart, sexy picture, and five-day weather forecast was an enticement to step into the forest, and once I was two or three breadcrumbs down the path, the witches had me, I was in their oven. Most of life's temptations go way back; they're ancient and perennial, and one is warned about them in one's youth, but this temptation had appeared from nowhere.

My girlfriend at the time, another journalist, was working in a room across the hall. I yelled and ran in with my laptop, set it down, and read the story aloud to her while she perused it on the screen. "He snapped," I said. "He finally lost his mind."

There had been signs this moment was coming. "I have a

plan," he had said to me one night, and then he'd described for me a vile project that, he said, another divorced father had agreed to back with money. Would I come in as a partner too? The scheme involved building a private offshore facility, possibly in the Philippines or Peru, where American men could impregnate local young women who had sold off their legal interests in the progeny. "We won't need these silly women then," Clark said. "Fathers will have sole title to their children."

"Did you come up with this idea? Of title?"

"It's perfectly workable and it solves the problem. Women who want to be mothers without men are able to do so with donated sperm. Why shouldn't men have a similar alternative? I do have a point."

But a point was all he had. He was like this sometimes: a creature of perfect reason whose conclusions were nonetheless insane. His hateful proposed breeding program not only treated women as dispensable, as hatcheries, it assumed that children were interchangeable. I thought it was his very own Snooks he missed? Wrong. What he missed, I'd come to see, was fatherhood itself, and fatherhood as he defined it meant control. Exclusive control, if he could swing it. On another occasion, in another phone call, he'd told me that Argentina—or was it Chile?—offered safe harbor to American fathers who fled there with their children.

Maybe he was in South America now. I considered calling the FBI but decided to wait a day, sure Clark would turn up, since how could a Rockefeller ever hope to vanish underground, and why would one want to, especially in Chile? He'd repent of his error, hire a top lawyer, negotiate his freedom, and publicly rehabilitate himself. He'd show humility. Adopt a cause.

The next morning I read that the manhunt had intensified. I also read that the Rockefellers, through one of those "family spokesmen" that big-shot clans always have at their disposal, were denying that Clark was one of them. What cowards these people were, I thought, forsaking their own blood out of fear of scandal. "This is disgusting. It's bullshit," I told my girlfriend. She nodded in apparent solidarity and then excused herself to do some work. I turned on the TV news and phoned my mother. "You're watching all this?" I said to her. "You've heard?"

"It sounds like your friend was a phony, Walt."

"They're pulling something," I said. "It's a big family. It has factions. He's from the black sheep side or something."

"That's just silly."

"Maybe he's illegitimate."

"Oh, darling."

A few hours later a German name came out. I holed up with my computer in my office and sent my girlfriend off to eat alone while I read every report that I could find. About Clark's origins they all agreed—his German mother and brother were giving interviews—and yet the story made no sense. Then again, nothing had ever made sense with Clark, and in just this crazy way. In truth, I'd always marked him as a phony, but only because they were all phonies, his type, particularly the normal-acting ones who people liked to describe as "down to earth." Clark's extravagant, emphatic phoniness demonstrated his honesty, I felt. Earth? He simply had no use for it. Nor would I, if I were born with wings.

What a perfect mark I'd been. Rationalizing, justifying, imagining. I'd worked as hard at being conned by him as he had at conning me. I wasn't a victim; I was a collaborator. I'd been taught when I was young, and had learned for myself as I grew older, that deception creates a chain reaction: two lies protecting the one that came before, and on and on and on. Now I was learning something new; how *being* deceived, and not wishing to admit it, could proliferate into a kind of madness too. The revelations came swiftly after that, but none of them staggered me as the first ones had. The reports of Clark's suspected role in a two-decades-old murder hardly fazed me; by then I expected nothing less of him. My girl-friend, who lived mostly in New York, slipped back there, away from Montana, during this interlude. My kids showed up on alternating weekends, but I was mentally distant.

I called my mother to apologize. She'd been right about Clark, and her son had been an idiot. All she cared about was that his daughter had been found safe.

"I'm curious if he killed those people," she said.

"Of course he did."

"Did you ever have suspicions?"

Did I? As a college English major, I'd learned the phrase "suspension of disbelief," but with Clark you *contributed* belief, wiring it from your personal account into the account you held with him. He showed you a hollow tree; you added the bees. He slipped you the phone number of the president; you added the voice that would greet you if you dialed it and the faces of the Secret Service agents who would show up at your door a few days later. He gave you an envelope with a check inside; you filled in the amount.

Magazine stories were being written and friends from the press were calling, wanting anecdotes. I spoke off the record and not at length, still constrained by vestigial loyalty. You don't hear that someone you've known for years is bad and instantly pivot to dump on them; it feels opportunistic and debased, a breach of faith with the concept of faith itself. We're brought up to trust and could hardly function otherwise. The cop who pulls us over to write a ticket must be a cop because he wears the uniform; the bank teller to whom we hand our paycheck is depositing it, not stealing it, because he works behind a marble counter; the nurse who places our newborn in our arms is really a nurse because she's holding our baby, and our baby is our baby because she's holding it. When trust is abused, the need for it persists.

Trust was crumbling everywhere just then. In August and September 2008, Lehman Brothers, the Bernie Madoff investment fund, the market in mortgages and their fancy derivatives were all exposed as Clark Rockefellers writ large. Who were the Lehman brothers, anyway? Letterhead fodder. And what were mortgage-backed securities, those infamous instruments of mass insolvency? They brought to mind the old joke about the man who asks what's holding up the world and is told that it rests on the broad back of an elephant. But what supports the elephant? Another elephant. And under that one? Elephants the whole way down. No wonder Clark, when he was in a pinch, sought to camouflage himself on Wall Street. A swindler alone is nothing but a crook, but a swindler surrounded by thousands of other swindlers is a dealer-broker.

It took several months for my bond with Clark to dissipate, but once it did I resolved to write about him. I remember the very day. I was sitting in the same office at the same desk where we'd arranged the delivery of Shelby. I had a new girlfriend by then, Amanda, a writer from Los Angeles, who'd come back to Livingston with me after a winter of romance in California that left me homesick for my kids. Out in the hallway Charlie was shooting free throws at a mesh hoop I'd mounted above a doorway. Maisie was blasting her Hello Kitty boom box and pretending to read *Tom Sawyer*, my idea, while actually reading a teenage vampire saga, popular culture's idea. Amanda was trying to nap using earplugs, resting up after our frolic in Saint Louis, where a movie of one of my novels was being shot. We'd hung out with George Clooney, a terrifying charmer, and had even been asked up to his hotel room—an invitation I'd declined for both of us in the interest of keeping our relationship and preserving my tenuous sobriety. On my desk was a fresh white legal pad with the optimistic heading "Projects." Magazine writing, my major source of income, was swiftly dissolving in an online acid bath of unpaid content. I needed a book idea.

Sorry, Clark. You asked for it, old sport. You knew who I was, and deep down I knew who you were, even if I played dumb there for a time—so dumb that I didn't realize I was playing, which, looking back, was a fairly cunning strategy. You were material. Surprise, surprise. Look in your wallet; it's empty. Now look in mine.

SANDRA BOSS'S TESTIMONY TOOK all day, and before she could be cross-examined the clock ran out. My daughter lost interest about halfway through and started glancing at her turned-off phone, anxious to resume her online social life. Her lapse of focus disappointed me, but I blamed modernity, not her. The center had not only failed to hold, it had ceased to exist as a viable idea, even as a memory. We hurried away from downtown to beat the traffic and drove up and over the pass into the Valley where Charlie and Maggie were staying at a hotel. Maggie had remarried a few months earlier. Her new husband mixed sound for the pop singer John Mayer; Maisie was set to see him that night at a big group dinner. Dad bids a murder trial, Mom bids rock and roll; Mom wins by a point, or maybe several. It was fine. It was life's reciprocating engine of displeasure and acceptance, imperfection and compromise. Clark had rejected this cycle; he inclined toward absolutism. He'd pursued another program: triumph. Salty soup, mashed potatoes, and bread again for him tonight. I'd heard that he didn't mind prison, that it suited him.

"So what did you think?" I asked my daughter. I could

see the hotel up ahead, its spotlit palm trees, the valet line of German sports cars and convertibles. The trial was set to wind up in a few days, but then I would have to hunker down and write and possibly look for a way to speak with Clark, particularly if he wound up safely jailed. I wouldn't see my kids for weeks.

"It's surprising how much like TV it is," she said. "It's a little more boring, but that's the only difference. Also, I think he'll get off. Too circumstantial." She pulled the last rubber band out of her hair and shook it out smooth and straight and long, getting ready for her rock-star dinner. "Did you like him, Dad?" she asked me.

I gave this some thought. One owes this to a child. They think about everything, the world is new to them, and the effort they make deserves to be returned.

"I did," I said.

"Why?"

"He was smart. I like smart people. Plus, he has a certain hypnotic way of talking. It pulls you along and lulls you and draws you in."

"You're lucky he didn't kill you too," she said. She leaned over and kissed my cheek but barely grazed it—her custom lately, no contact, the gesture only—then got out of the car and walked toward the hotel. Maggie and Charlie were waiting there. They waved. Their waves might have been for Maisie, but I waved back at them. I don't think they noticed, though. They were too far away.

THIRTEEN

WE ALL UNDERSTAND that you can't predict the future, but getting to know an old friend, however perversely, through his murder trial, reveals a truth less commonly acknowledged: you can't predict the past. It can change at any time. As Balian called his last few witnesses and reporters placed their bets, anticipating a hung jury, it occurred to me that my life's road had forked behind me. When fresh information discredits past perceptions, the underlying memories remain but they no longer hold their old positions; you're left to draw a new map with displaced landmarks. You thought you were found but you realize that you were lost, and someday you may discover that you're lost now.

This distressing idea solidified for me when one of Clark's New Hampshire neighbors, a blueberry farmer named Christopher Kuzma, repeated a number of stories Clark had told him that I had once swallowed as readily as he had. The one about the jet propulsion lab in Canada, whose existence Clark sought to render credible by giving Kuzma an arm patch from a Shuttle mission and by sending him e-mails containing photos of a satellite. The one about harvesting wild honey. The one about having influential contacts inside the British government. Kuzma's best story, though, was new to me. On a trip to New York City, while touring the Metropolitan Museum of Art, Clark got on his phone in front of Kuzma and ordered the museum to return several multimillion-dollar paintings that he'd supposedly lent the institution. One might have been a Rothko. Kuzma wasn't sure.

Balian concluded with a question intended to show that Clark had hidden from Kuzma his links to California. "Did he ever mention the names of any other cities that he was connected to in the United States?"

"Umm, Montana, at one point . . ."

My sinuses drained, an effect of spiking adrenaline. I'd heard here and there that Clark sometimes referred to a ranch he owned somewhere—in Wyoming, according to one source, near a spread belonging to Dick Cheney, who Clark said had asked him to marry one of his daughters and was crestfallen when he married Sandy instead. This source said Clark seemed fairly knowledgeable about the ranch's operations, the machinery required, the irrigation methods. I was sure this knowledge came from me. Among the very few questions Clark ever asked me were several about western agriculture. One, I recalled, was exceedingly specific. "You mentioned an off-road utility vehicle that you haul tools and supplies in? Its name again?"

"A Gator," I replied. "Like 'Alligator.'"

"Manufactured by?"

"John Deere."

"A John Deere Gator. Excellent. I'm buying one, Walter, for my Cornish place tomorrow. Can it go in the water?"

"Above its axles? I don't quite understand."

"Does it convert to a watercraft?" he asked.

"You're thinking of something I think they call a 'Duck.'"

"A 'Duck.' Very good. I'll buy one of those as well."

The man was a brain tick. He crawled into your hair and fed on your life through a puncture in your scalp. Montana. If he had ever showed up there, the first thing he would have done, the record indicated, was ask to be addressed by a new name. Security. Privacy. You understand, Walter. The name would have had a western, campfire quality to go with its aroma of eastern breeding. Buck Vanderbilt? Slim Whitney? Maybe he would have styled himself a Bush, a lost Bush sent packing by his Texas elders for setting fire to his private school or running over a child in downtown Houston. Buddy Bush. Buffalo Bush.

Bailey's cross-examination of Kuzma followed the tart,

sardonic, established approach that seemed to play poorly with the jury. Mock the witness for tolerating Clark's blarney, implying that the witness was full of it himself. Had Kuzma ever seen the private jet that Clark claimed to have at his disposal? No. Had Clark mentioned Kevin Costner? Yes. "And if you pardon my crudity," said Bailey, who'd already pardoned himself for it long ago, "on another level you kind of thought he was full of crap, right?"

"No."

This answer convinced me of Kuzma's honesty. So did his guileless response when Bailey asked him why he "hung around" with the defendant. "Because he was entertaining," Kuzma said. I would have answered the same way. Clark was diverting, and now we all knew why—because there was something he wanted to divert us from, a grave marked with an X on our new maps.

Vertigo. That sense of falling while standing still, that illusion of standing still while falling. The relevant movie reference was also *Vertigo*, about a man who falls in love with a woman who doesn't exist. I felt it most keenly the day of Kuzma's testimony because it might have been me there on the stand retelling some of the same tales and reminding the combative, literal Bailey that True and False are not the salient categories when it comes to life outside the courtroom. Try Lively and Dull. Exciting and Exhausting. Intriguing and Tedious. No wonder the press was expecting a hung jury—not only was the evidence circumstantial, so was the defendant. He was the sum of the stories that he'd told and the reactions they'd produced. To be a murderer one must be a person, but other than the German passport that the police were lucky to have found, there was no hard proof of this in Clark's case.

I glanced at them sitting up sober in their box, the jurors who'd soon be required to pass judgment on someone the rest of us had just let pass, concerned with our amusement, not his veracity. They were wearing the earnest masks of civic duty, but after all they'd heard these past few weeks—the adventures of a film noir baronet; how to succeed in business without really existing; the country husband from outer space—my guess was that they found Clark entertaining too.

FOURTEEN

THE NIGHT AFTER Balian made his closing statement, an impassioned reprise of his opening
remarks that was largely delivered from behind
Clark's chair and ended on a potent note of apparently
long-suppressed, sarcastic contempt ("Yes, I said he's a master
manipulator. I have never said he was a master murderer"),
I rented a movie that I'd been meaning to watch and Clark
might have seen in one of his classes. Its English title is *Purple
Noon*. Its original French title is *Plein soleil*. Made in 1960,
the year before Christian Gerhartsreiter was born, it is the

first film adaptation of Patricia Highsmith's *The Talented Mr. Ripley.*

Alain Delon plays the social-climbing shape-shifter. He stabs rich Philippe Greenleaf (Dickie in the novel) while they're out sailing in the Mediterranean, dumps his body into the sea, and then goes about impersonating him, concealing the crime by forging his victim's signature on some letters written on his typewriter. Ripley sends them, postmarked Italy, to Greenleaf's family. (The postcards supposedly written by Linda Sohus and sent from Paris after her disappearance appeared to be Clark's homage to Ripley's ploy.) Many other evasions and maneuvers follow, including the murder of Greenleaf's snoopy college chum, but just when Ripley thinks he's in the clear, the body turns up in a freak way, snagged on the sailboat's anchor cable, and the game is up. This isn't how Highsmith's book ends. In the novel, Ripley gets away. He returns in a sequel, *Ripley Under Ground,* married to a woman of means and involved in a plot to counterfeit the work of a painter who committed suicide.

Some people kill for love and some for money, but Clark, I'd grown convinced, had killed for literature. To be a part of it. To live inside it. To test it in the most direct ways possible. This wasn't a motive most juries would find intelligible, and when I'd tried it out one day on Balian, walking beside him in the hall as he pushed his rolling file cart toward the elevators, he awarded me not a flicker of agreement, let alone comprehension. I understood. He was seeking a conviction, not an epiphany or a literary exegesis.

But I'd already had one: even as a fraud, Clark was a fraud. He'd never had an idea of his own, not about how to speak or how to dress or which science fiction TV show to obsess about or how to cover up a murder. He was wholly, impeccably derivative. On the *Today* show, "the aficionado of station wagons" spoke of an old Ford "woody" with "pop-up headlights" in which he'd taken those childhood vacations to Mount Rushmore and other spots that he never really visited but claimed to recall more clearly than his own name. After the clip was shown in court, Ellen Sohus, John's sister, revealed to me that Clark was, in fact, describing the vintage station wagon, a quite distinctive model, used by her own family when they went on holidays. As for two television programs he'd boasted of associations with—*Alfred Hitchcock Presents*, the 1980s version, and *Star Trek: The Next Generation*—one was a subpar quasi-remake, the other a sequel (one of whose innovations was the "Holodeck," the Starship *Enterprise*'s onboard generator of elaborate virtual realities). Even Snooks, his daughter's pet name, was borrowed, lifted from the child of a family he'd known back in Connecticut.

Everything was mimicked, appropriated, sampled, down to the haircut he copied from the Chandler men, the fancied ranch he took from me, and the markers of Wasp culture that he skimmed, I'm convinced, from a best-selling book that hit the stores months after he reached America: *The Official Preppy Handbook: The first guide to* The *Tradition, Mannerisms, Etiquette, Dress Codes, The Family. How to*

Be Really Top Drawer. Its caption-filled front cover was his tip sheet, at least in matters of footwear and shirt selection. "The Crucial Element: Top-Siders, Loafers, Tassel. Cuffs a must. The Sock Controversy . . ." "The Virtues of Pink and Green." It was marketed as a humor book, but Clark, whose immunity to facetious irony was, looking back, the diagnostic key I missed, never got the joke. Which didn't harm him, as it happened, because he circulated among the snotty targets of the joke: the American gentry, itself a desperate reproduction of the British gentry, a prettified warrior class all spiffed up with the spoils of its conquests. The very last of which, of course (achieved with the help of its Yankee allies), was Germany.

Buried under all the shams, the shame. Germany—it lost. But Clark liked to ride with winners. There is only one chapel in all America, or in all the world, where General George Patton is rendered in stained glass standing in the turret of a tank ringed by the names of captured German towns: the chapel where Clark chose to worship in San Marino while using the surname of a British sailor who was also a hero of World War Two.

Lebensraum, the word Clark couldn't resist even though it risked giving him away. It meant room to spread out and manifest one's destiny. Hitler sought it but failed to get it. Clark, the copycat, resumed the campaign on a minor level and succeeded, in America. Soon he was acting like he owned the place. He learned it responded well to being owned. Clubs closed to most of us stowed his wet umbrellas and counted out the ice cubes in his drinks. Skyscraper restaurants ushered him to tables with radiant, titanic, plunging views. The art of American postwar splash and swagger hung confident and colossal on his walls. His surname meant "Don't ask. Now step aside." It was quite an endeavor, quite an operation.

The problem was that it was all done undercover, with borrowed gestures, borrowed language, borrowed clothes, and borrowed tropes, meaning that Clark, despite appearances, never truly rose at all; except for the odd *Lebensraum*, his real self never even broke the surface. Once he submerged himself in the persona that he began rehearsing at the Savios, the only progress left to him was downward, deeper into concealment and imitation. But deeper concealment required deeper secrets. He went looking for some and found, inevitably, the deepest one of all, and, to a certain type of mind—his type—the most prestigious: murder.

But where could he borrow a murder plot?

From books and movies, where he borrowed most things.

But where could he borrow his victims?

From right next door, where later he'd borrow the iced-tea supplies for his festive Trivial Pursuit night.

It was two in the morning when the movie ended. I had to be at the courthouse by nine A.M., which meant I had to hit the road by seven. The jury might come back at at any time, and the prosecution's powerful closing had changed the betting among the trial watchers, convincing them that a guilty verdict loomed. "He's gotten away with it for twenty-eight years," Balian told the jurors, whose faces wore a grim, determined cast. "He thinks he's smarter than everyone. Do you remember what he told Ed Savio when he voted? He [Savio] said, 'How did you vote? You don't have a license?' What did he [Clark] say? 'People are so stupid.' He thinks people are so stupid."

And so we were. The trial had proved Clark right, at least about the people who'd known him best: bankers, brokers, degree-holding professionals, and several published writers, including me. I lay in bed next to the open *Ripley* novel and the computer on which I'd watched the movie. Clark, a composite being of ink and celluloid, utterly transparent to me now, had cloaked himself in the stuff of my own literacy. The instant familiarity I felt with him—this consummate immigrant, this immigrant with a vengeance—was my familiarity with my own culture. Of course he'd fooled me. Of course he'd held me spellbound. He spoke from inside my own American mind.

IN THE WINDOWLESS LIMBO of the ninth-floor's hallway, waiting for a verdict that might take days, I stood eating Fritos and gossiping with Frank Girardot while Clark's attorneys paced and used their phones, ignoring each other and looking miffed, as though they'd already concluded the case was lost and had traded bitter words of blame. I had gotten to know them a bit during the trial. Denner was the cool, recessive strategist, hooded and impassive in the courtroom but brimming with cheerful blarney in the hall, forever reminding me that he'd gone to Yale and ribbing me—ha, ha—about Princeton. The insults depended on hoary, in-group stereo-types that I would have thought had died out fifty years ago, but apparently they'd lived on in Denner's New England, the rarefied snob heaven that Clark had travestied and finally humiliated. I sensed that defending him embarassed Den-ner, who, rumor had it, had pushed for an insanity plea. I doubted that a loss would bother him, but I suspected it would crush his partner. Bailey, the lantern-jawed, rhyming barrister, had literally changed complexion over the trial, turning redder by the day. His ritual "Good morning"s to the jury were being returned with a smirking choral disdain that seemed ominously uniform. Not once had the jurors shown any visible interest in his insinuations about Linda, the allegedly dangerous Dungeons and Dragons enthusiast.

The one-hour warning to the press that the jury had reached a verdict came to me via a phone call from Girardot while I was eating at a taco stand on Cesar Chavez Avenue, a couple of miles from the courthouse. The men around me, workers on their breaks, reminded me of the two Latino jurors whom I'd been scrutinizing during the trial: the big fellow with the hat and the dark shades and a younger guy, just as broad and muscular, who sat beside him, sometimes asking questions, and seemed to be under his sway. I'd assumed they would vote as one, and until recently, having profiled them in my callow way as hostile to the powers that be, I'd expected them to vote for an acquittal. Then, a few days ago, something switched in me. I saw the dark-glasses man, chewing gum as usual, train his shielded eyes toward Clark, who was working his co-investigator act—Sherlock, the accidentally accused—and hold the gaze for five seconds, ten, fifteen. Clark didn't look up at him—too busy scribbling, pretending to sort and analyze the clues. Two worlds were meeting, but one was unaware of it—the world for which the other had never existed except as a faceless labor pool. I knew then what would happen and told Girardot, who understood his city better than I did and wasn't convinced I'd drawn the right conclusion.

The defendant strolled into the courtroom, took his seat, crossed his sockless ankles, squared his narrow shoulders, and pleasantly, politely, faced the judge, wearing a faintly downturned smile in which I detected a coiled confidence; the smile would turn suddenly upward for the cameras at the moment of exoneration, creating an arresting bit of footage. Denner leaned back in his chair and trained his eyes on an unseen, abstract object floating beween him and the stenographer, while Bailey threw an arm around the client who, according to a courthouse loiterer, he'd once referred to in the hallway as "our Bavarian prick."

Endings. You long for them, speculating, anticipating, but as they draw near their magic dims: just another event occurring inside a room, its thermostat set to a certain temperature, its lights adjusted to a certain brightness, and, in the adjacent rooms, people who don't care, preoccupied with endings of their own. I pitied Clark as the verdict was read aloud and time neither slowed nor swerved, just dripped along. He'd fashioned a life of cinematic moments, of victims' startled faces, of stressful getaways, of white-gloved welcomes into gorgeous parlors, of ringing phones that must not be picked up. Once, a few weeks after the murder, a policeman rang the guesthouse doorbell, perhaps before all the gore had been sponged up. Tight spot. No time to think. But Clark surpassed himself. He answered the door naked, completely naked, proclaiming himself a nudist when asked to dress, as though he were resisting on religious grounds. The flustered policeman excused himself and said he'd stop by later. Clark shut the door, resuming the form he took behind shut doors. Reveals, dissolves, blackouts. He controlled the final cut. Then the studio took away his picture.

"Guilty."

Clark nodded.

The deputies led him out. Ellen Sohus, across the aisle from me, rose from her seat and relaxed her strict perimeter of inviolable pensiveness and torment to receive congratulations and condolences from reporters, lawyers, clerks, and strangers. Balian hurried away to do a press conference, his movements unconsciously elegant and preening, as though he'd traded souls with a white pony.

The jurors departed through their private door, back to their closed room. I'd speak to a few of them later that day and learn that they reached their decision easily; the book bags around the skull had cinched the case for them. One middle-aged woman who'd studied Clark throughout had observed him talking to himself and thought "some mental issue was going on." The mustache-and-sunglasses man, a truck driver, scoffed at the Parisian postcards ruse along with Clark's whole repertoire of tricks, implying that he'd seen them all before, or at least some version of them, out on the road and around the neighborhood. "You meet guys like that. It's not that strange," he said. "Being rich is probably nice—I wouldn't know—but it doesn't make you smart."

Feeling smart at Clark's expense, a gratification few had ever experienced, was the emotion of the hour. Once people had savored it, they started leaving. The trial's improvised family was breaking up. The *LA Times* reporters crossed the plaza to their paper's massive downtown headquarters, a building I'd passed a dozen times that month without seeing anyone go in or out. The impossibly true-blue Balian, whom my daughter had melted over on sight, and whom I expected to hear of next as a high municipal office holder, headed off to watch his child's baseball game. Denner wrapped Ellen Sohus in a hug of hard-to-parse but genuine-looking feeling, his briefcase held high behind her back. I said goodbye to a pregnant German TV producer whose baby was due the next day. I didn't want to leave yet. I felt like a barfly after closing time who's still a few beers short of stiff. Some enormous formality had been concluded, but only on Clark's side, not on mine. Plus there was too much schadenfreude around; the air was thick with sticky karmic residue. I mentioned this to Girardot on my way out—that I felt like I'd just taken pleasure in a stoning. Maybe we could grab a bite and talk? He couldn't; too busy. He'd just thrown on his tie to do a spot for a TV morning show. The technicians and interviewer stood nearby, impatient for tape.

"Why don't you just go visit him?" he said.

This tripped me up. I didn't understand. Clark's unavailability for visits was a long-established fact. Denner was adamant: no press, no friends. I'd asked him a year ago and then a month ago, a week before the trial. Not a chance.

"They convicted his ass," Girardot said. "It's different now. Nobody cares, believe me. He's on his own. Plus, I hear he's firing his lawyers. You may as well try." I told him I'd call him later that week, or possibly the next day if he were free, and we could discuss the matter further. This made him grin. Reporters, where he came from, weren't further discussers. They acted; they plunged in.

"This is all you have to do," he said, and I knew as he said it, knew inwardly and sadly but with the strange exhilaration that comes of sacrificing pride to clarity, that I'd learned nothing of value at the trial. I was the risk to myself I'd always been, as readily intrigued and led as ever. "Just go online and put in a request—it's Men's Central Jail, Department of Corrections; Google it, they have a Web site—and I bet you see him this weekend, if you want. You can set it up now, on your phone. It's all online."

FIFTEEN

THERE WEREN'T MANY men in the line outside the jail; mostly it was young women, scores of them, most of them with children, quite a few with babies. I wanted to tell them to run away, and fast, and remind them that moving toward danger was perverse. The men they were here to see weren't worth it, particularly not the boyfriends and the husbands. Ditch them while you still can, I wanted to say. But what did I know? My errand this Sunday morning was a one-time thing and purely voluntary, experimental. Surprisingly, I was underdressed. Maybe a lot of the women had come from church, or maybe they

were headed to church afterward, but they had on their finest. I was wearing a T-shirt. I thought it would help me
blend in. I wasn't thinking straight. If you're free and you
visit a prison, you don't blend in, and no one is looking at
you anyway.

Our meeting started awkwardly. I hadn't seen him from
the front for years, and here he was on display for me, framed
in a window of plate glass or plastic, seated in a long row
of other men in identical loose blue smocks that made them
look like hospital orderlies. The heavy, beige, old-fash-
ioned plastic phone receivers that allowed for conversation
through the glass didn't switch on for a few minutes, forcing
us to mouth inaudible greetings while gazing at each other
from such close range that I could see light-colored, flecked
irregularities in the iris of Clark's left eye. The proximity
felt uncomfortably intimate, and the temptation to stare was
irresistible, so I compensated with a broad smile that felt
falser and fiercer by the second. To keep it fresh, I shifted
my lips and cheeks. Clark approached the problem differently. He tilted his head up at a submissive angle and fixed
me with a dreamy, unblinking look that seemed sweet at
first, then mildly terrifying. The standoff grew absurd. The
planes and curves and hollows of his face became abstract,
like a scaled-down Easter Island monolith, while my strug-
gle to keep my own face meaningful felt animalistic and
insane. Worse, a feeling of competition developed.

"You're my very first visitor," he said when the phones
came on. He asked after my children, now a creepy cour-

tesy, and then, with two other prisoners crowding him from their adjacent conversation stations, he pushed his pale forehead up against the glass and asked for my help finding a literary agent. His new novel, written in pencil while in prison, was eight hundred thousand words long, he told me, and covered the entire swath of European history between the end of World War One and the 1960s. He outlined the story for me. It sounded boring, a monolith of insufferable pedantry born of unconscious aggression toward its readers, whoever Clark imagined them to be. I lied, and said I'd look into the agent thing. He seemed to believe me, which I found interesting. Pathological liars, I'd heard somewhere, could not be lied to, but I'd soon learn that the opposite was true, that they were avid consumers, not just producers.

I'd arrived with questions, endless questions, but I put off asking them, preferring to let him run. The scratched slab between us seemed to magnify and fix him, turning him into a specimen, an exhibit, and bringing out the cold researcher in me. Prison, he said, had finally freed him as a writer, both by forcing him to write by hand ("the interference of screen and keyboard" had cramped his imagination, he'd concluded) and by minimizing interruptions. He said he particularly liked composing sonnets, both Petrarchan and Elizabethan, and he asked if I'd send him a book on sonnet structure or, if a book were too expensive, I could print out an article from the Internet. I promised a book.

This seemed to energize him. He propped his hands under his chin and faced me squarely; the crow's-feet around his pink-rimmed eyes appeared to be packed with fine black dust or soot. Did I know of "a good one-volume Shakespeare in paperback?" Not offhand, I said, but I could find one. "Walter, that would be wonderful," he said. That's when his face changed, like a creature in a fairy tale. It softened, blurred, grew candle-lit, adoring, the face of a good little German boy at Christmas. "Truly," he said, "I would be forever grateful."

I pulled back from the trance. It helped that my right leg was numb; I must have been sitting tensely on my chair. Two spots down from me a teenage girl was pressing her squalling baby up to the glass, tilting it upright hospital-nursery style. I'd seen her in a kiosk in the waiting room swiping a credit card in a machine that transferred funds to inmates. I understood now: prison walls aren't solid. They're penetrable by persuasion, by attraction, which passes through them like gamma rays. The inmates beam their wills into the world, adjusting the intensities and wavelengths, tuning the dial until they get results.

That soft, glowing face Clark had summoned out of nowhere must have worked on someone else once, but when and on whom I didn't want to know. I resolved not to send the books; not a chance. His magic had to be thwarted, or it might spread.

It was time to ask questions. I started with the most general: Why had he spent his life deceiving people, and why should anyone believe him now?

"Consider me a drug addict," he said. "A drug addict

who's recovered. Not literally, of course; I don't even drink coffee. But hiding and lying are just what addicts do."

The answer felt pat and tailored to its audience, me, the abstaining alcoholic, but I had to admire how quickly he'd come up with it. Not a pause, not a twitch, and full eye contact throughout. In what parallel, sped-up dimension did he perform his calculations and how did he send them so swiftly back to this one?

I asked him next about his art, his gorgeous collection of Motherwells and Rothkos. "Fakes," he said. "All fakes, Walter. But very good ones." He gave me the name of a man who, so he claimed, had pressed the paintings on him in the belief that their possession by a Rockefeller would provide them with "provenance" and allow them to be sold as genuine. He said the man was living in Peru now and that they'd met at an "Old Masters cocktail hour." Then, from a hidden fold in his green prison smock, he produced a scrap of paper—tiny, the torn-off corner of a page—and a pencil stub barely long enough to hold. He wrote the man's name down and held it to the glass, a trick for bypassing the phones, which, he'd confided to me earlier, were bugged. Because I'd been forbidden to bring a notebook, I had to memorize the name, and I wondered why Clark was so eager for me to have it. Did he want me to contact the man? I cocked my head, inviting him to explain, in code if necessary.

Instead, he made another request of me. The paintings, along with all his other possessions—most notably, some "very nice old furniture" and "all Snooks's drawings"—

were stored, he said, in a locker in Baltimore that he could no longer afford to pay the rent on. Would I be so kind as to keep them in Montana while he appealed his case? It wouldn't cost me anything; a few of the antiques were going to auction soon and he'd reimburse me from the proceeds. If I wished to, I could also sell the paintings. They were worthless in themselves, he said, but perhaps their status as "Clark Rockefellers" (he spoke the words flatly, without irony) would lend them appeal for a certain type of buyer. I might get two thousand dollars apiece for them. Or I could keep them. It was up to me. The main thing was Snooks's little drawings. And her toys. Would I think about it?

I said I would. I was humoring him; the whole idea was both infuriating and mad. Though maybe it was appropriately mad. As a souvenir of our relationship, a phony Rothko might be nice. I could hang the thing in my office above my desk, a totem, a trophy, a conversation piece. There were all kinds of closure, most of them illusory, but this might be the rare exception. The notion, once again, was growing on me. I had to stop it.

I'd lost track of time. We only had thirty minutes and I still hadn't asked about the murder. There seemed no point. I'd fantasized on the drive over that I might get a confession— headline news!—but now this seemed unlikely; Clark was still portraying the man I'd known, a patrician Lotos Club member, unceremoniously displaced. Also, I was shy. I'd never asked such a question of a person and wasn't certain I could form the words. This bothered me. It seemed cowardly and weak. But what bothered me more was that if I didn't ask, Clark would discern my weakness and might exploit it, in the psychic realm, if not the physical. Before today's visit this might have seemed absurd—an astral assault conducted through the ether—but now that we were head to head, possibly near enough to generate crackles of blue static, I worried. I'd erred in coming; I wasn't a materialist. My faith in glass partitions wasn't strong enough. I blamed my years as a Mormon, a ghostly sect rife with otherworldly folklore—golden plates translated by second sight, plagues of crickets stopped by prayer—but I also blamed my mother's recent death, which had opened holes in my reality. I'd seen an unusual number of crows since losing her, messenger birds that appeared at Poe-like moments, when I was alone and she was on my mind. Symbolic spoked wheels kept turning up as well, in songs, in poems, in art. They seemed to be versions of the Bighorn Medicine Wheel, an ancient Native American rock altar located on a mountain in Wyoming, that I was heading off to visit the day I got the news of her collapse.

"Tell me about the murder."

There, I'd done it. I'd shown the devil I was brave.

"Oh, that," Clark said. "Well, there's not much I can say. I'm innocent. It wasn't me. That jury, you see, never liked me very much. They would have convicted me of anything. The Kennedy assassination. Anything. It was all a mistake. They'll have to overturn it. I'm absolutely confident they will."

"So who killed John Sohus?"

Out came the secret pencil. He didn't use it right away. First, he denigrated his attorneys, particularly Denner, who he said was too old and frail to practice law. He lowered his voice conspiratorially and leaned closer to the glass. "He may have had a stroke during the trial." The charge was horrible and patently false; the act of speaking it left a ratty ring around his mouth. His next target was Linda Sohus. She'd killed her husband, he said, and fled the country, probably to Mexico. "We've turned up some leads," he said. We. The pronoun fit. There were many of him, all sharing the same skull. The psychotic "we." He started writing. Block letters again, like on a ransom note. He held up the scrap of paper so I could read them:

"Occult Witch."

I spoke the words aloud, for the bugged phone. I wasn't supposed to, which was why I did it.

"You're a very good guesser," he said. "That's what she was."

We'd run out of drama but not out of time; the minutes must have subdivided themselves. He used this to his favor, turning off the nastiness and smoothing his way toward a less disgusting exit by talking about his hopes for an appeal and the chance that he might see his daughter again, somehow. He wrote her a letter every day, he said. He didn't send them, but someday she'd get all of them. It might be soon. The trial had been a farce. The verdict would be overturned.

"So this is all temporary?" I swept my hand around.

"Absolutely," he said. "A minor inconvenience."

I had another question, a writer's question, imprecise and difficult to phrase but essential, I felt, if I could just define it. "I'm curious how you see people," I said. "I'm curious what your career—your life, I mean, you know, succeeding as an impostor—has taught you about—"

"What?"

"Human nature, I guess."

"I really don't understand."

"I'm making it too complicated. What is it you look for in people? What's the key? The key to manipulating people?"

He almost laughed. "Too easy. That's too easy." Then nothing. A long, bored sigh. To make me beg.

"Fine, but I want to hear it from the expert."

He liked this; it drew fresh black ink into his pupils.

"I think you know," he said.

"I'm asking you, though."

"Vanity, vanity, vanity," he said.

But it still wasn't over. I couldn't make it end. We talked about prison life. I asked about the food. He told me that the trick was insisting on eating kosher. Finally, right before the phones turned off—I still don't know how he timed it, but he did—he thanked me for coming and asked when I'd be back.

SIXTEEN

H E KNEW BETTER than I did what I'd do next, not because he understood me personally—a conceited, reflexive belief of mine that turned out to be the source of the whole spell—but because he viewed me mechanically, *impersonally*, as a mind infatuated with its own energy.

From a purely epistemological standpoint, involving yourself in the life of a great liar, once you understand that he's a liar but go on seeking the truth from him, is a swan dive through a mirror into a whirlpool. In the past Clark had merely left me clueless, convincing me that he was someone he wasn't, but now that I knew to expect him to misinform me, he could drive me to the brink. On April 19, the night after our jailhouse conversation, I typed in the name he'd given me—the supposed art dealer who allegedly had supplied Clark with the fake paintings—along with "Peru," the hypothetical man's purported nation of residence. Out came a number of news stories in Spanish dating to 2012 about a Canadian expatriate who was accused of abducting his young daughter after pushing the mother of the girl to sign some sort of document or contract. I flashed back immediately to Clark's repellent scheme for breeding children in the Third World. He'd said he had a partner; it seemed I'd found him. In a video clip from a Peruvian news show, the mother of the missing child explicitly linked the Canadian man to Clark, whom she said she knew to be a murderer and appeared to fear. I remembered that when he had kidnapped Snooks, he'd prepared certain people for his absence by telling them he might visit Peru. To rendezvous with the Canadian? Now it looked that way. One reason the Internet fosters conspiracy theories is that its system of branching, crossing tunnels is shaped like paranoid reasoning itself, and once inside the shadow maze you find yourself tracking elusive glimmers of light that recede as fast as you can follow them. When I added the words "Fake" and "Rothko" to my search, I learned of an ongoing federal investigation centered on New York City's Knoedler Gallery, which had shut its doors a few years earlier after being sued by art collectors for peddling scores of bogus paintings (eighty million dollars' worth in all) by the very same abstract expressionists whose works I'd seen hanging in Clark's apartment. According to stories in the *New York Times*, *Vanity Fair*, and other publications, the gallery bought the paintings through the back door for a fraction of their value from a woman, Glafira Rosales, who claimed that they came from a so-called Mr. X, the secretive heir to a major family fortune. I immediately thought of Clark. Delving deeper, I came across an excerpt from Mark Seal's *The Man in the Rockefeller Suit*, a fascinating 2011 book about Clark's life and exploits, that showed he'd frequented the gallery, often pretending to shop for art. The Canadian art dealer also appeared, identified as a friend of Clark's, although the forgery scandal wasn't mentioned, likely because it hadn't fully emerged.

The hour of research that brought me to this point ballooned into days of frenzied investigation as I compared the timeline of the art fraud to Clark's movements through the years. The fake paintings started to hit the market in the early 1990s, not long after Clark married Sandy and stepped up his New York social life. The paintings stopped arriving at Knoedler, from what I could learn, around the time he was assembling his Chip Smith act and preparing to go underground with Snooks. Most damning of all, however, it seemed to me, was something Sandy's father, William Boss, had told me at lunch one day during the trial, that during one of his first meetings with his future son-in-law, Clark had asked him a peculiar question: How would a person sell a Rothko? Boss recalled being puzzled and having no answer. He knew very little about modern art and certainly wasn't in the market for any.

Merely by giving me the art dealer's name and hinting that he was engaged in shady business, Clark sent me into a labyrinth that recalled a nearly fatal adventure from Christmas Eve the year before. I was driving back to Montana through southern Idaho after a two-week visit to California, when it hit me that there was no Christmas tree at home. Maybe, I thought, I could cut one in the forest. It was almost midnight, the road was deserted, and in the car I happened to have a knife with a long, serrated blade that I imagined could saw through pitchy wood. I parked on the shoulder and walked down an embankment into the trees, which were mostly the same size, having been planted by the Forest Service to replace thousands that had died in a beetle infestation twenty years before. Thinking the job would take ten minutes, tops, I left my hat and mittens behind despite the windy, subzero weather.

I almost didn't make it back. I don't remember the moment I lost my way, but I do remember the moment afterward, when I gazed at the long, identical rows of trees laid out diagonally like veterans' tombstones and realized that no direction back looked any more promising than any other. I fought off panic and chose a path at random, which led me in a circle. I chose a new path and stuck to it until I crossed my own boot tracks in the snow. I needed a new plan, except I had none. My phone was in the car and I was freezing, starting to think like a hypothermia victim, shuttling between images of death and cozy fantasies of domestic warmth. One second I saw my body blue and stiff, the next I was piping pink frosting onto sugar cookies. I lingered in this state; when I was accidentally led to safety by the blast of a truck horn passing on the highway, I discovered that my car was no more than fifty yards away, screened by trees.

There were lessons there, perhaps too many to use, and they were of no help as I pursued the art fraud down the Web's forever-forking corridors. At the trial, Clark's attorneys had raised what I'd regarded as a good question, possibly the most baffling of them all: Why would a fugitive in a homicide case saddle himself with a surname so conspicuous that no one who met him could fail to spread the news? The question was offered as evidence of his innocence, but I saw it as either evidence of self-sabotage or of a penchant for arrogant effrontery. Now there was another explanation. His fabulous name had credentialed the phony art, and the art had returned the favor, credentialing him. Had the deal turned real profits? I sensed it had. But where had they gone? To Peru, perhaps, ahead of him.

I laid out some of these theories for James Ellroy when we finally met for our long-delayed dinner at his downtown hangout, Pacific Dining Car, a muffled warren of dim, connected rooms ideal for assignations and secret contract talks. Ellroy was already seated when I got there—a royal tipper amid a grateful staff—leaning back long-legged in his chair, all soaring, bald head and untucked Hawaiian shirt, an impeccably self-taught man of letters who looked like the

bail-bond king of Tijuana. Critics compared him to Raymond Chandler for his brutal hipster prose that preserved,
with Smithsonian Institution fidelity, the endangered American music of slurs and slams—racial, sexual, and every other
kind. What his writing concealed, though, was his decorous
soul; I'd come to him as a pilgrim several months ago, to tap
both his criminological erudition and his literary savvy, and
he'd received me with gentlemanly forbearance.

"You worried me on the phone today," he said, scratching his nose with a crooked pinkie finger. "You sounded
jittery." I already knew his opinion on Clark: a case of the
artistic temperament operating unrestrained by the stric-
tures of honest intellectual labor. To Ellroy, no force was
more destructive. Manson and Hitler, they were just the
biggies. The small fry were everywhere, all over town:
moochers, dopers, head cases, and creeps who'd come to
LA to act or write or play, couldn't cut it, made excuses,
made a half-assed creed of their excuses, pulled a break-in,
pimped their girl, and ended up in Griffith Park at night,
dumping the body of someone they'd bugged out on, or
being dumped by someone from their sick crowd.

"I know he's involved with this forgery scam," I said. "I
just don't have any way right now to prove it."

"Drop it," Ellroy said. "You never will."

"It's perfect, though. He's a forgery himself."

"That's beautiful. Drop it. It's a cruise to nowhere."

"How do you know?"

"He doesn't tell the truth."

Ellroy was a veteran of wild goose chases. His mother was murdered when he was ten, strangled after a night out in the bars of El Monte, California, a working-class town in the San Gabriel Valley that he'd described to me as "shitsville." In 1996 he published a memoir, *My Dark Places*, about his futile attempt to solve the crime decades after the case was closed. The fresh tips and leads he generated with the help of a retired detective were like the beehive in the hollow tree, beguiling but insubstantial.

Ellroy schooled me on LA over appetizers. Then the waiter brought our steaks: two sledge-hammer cuts of charred prime beef served on bare white plates.

"I'm going to see him in jail again," I said. "Maybe it's dumb, but I just want more from him."

"More perfidious psycho-grifter bullshit?" Ellroy was one far-out breed of do-right white guy. His nickname was "Dog," but his passion was Beethoven.

"Just more to work with," I said. "I'm still not satisfied."

"And that's your affliction, pal."

"Curiosity?"

"Wanting more. You want more than there is."

CLARK WAS BULGING WITH lies when I saw him two weeks later. They danced out of his mouth as though they'd been cooped up there and were glad for a chance to stretch their legs. The first one described the origins of the Canadian research lab, Jet Propulsion Physics, which bore such an ominous resemblance to Pasadena's Jet Propulsion Laboratory, where John Sohus was working when he was murdered. Clark denied there was any connection. It went like this, he said: he was writing a novel about a man of mystery, "Rex Bradley" (a "Thomas Crown–like adventurer—not a thief—a person of independent means"), and he wanted to give the character a profession. He put the question to Sandra, who came up with rocket scientist. He then invented a Web site for Bradley's company "as a way of exploring fictional ideas" and somehow the site leaped a metaphysical boundary and became, at least in the minds of others, a genuine defense contractor.

I'd come to confront him about the forgery scam, but since we were on the subject of the murder, I asked him why he'd left California that summer, so suddenly, and in the victim's truck. "Why does anyone leave Los Angeles?" he said. He answered his own question with a tale about a depressing meeting with Robert Wise, the director of *West Side Story*, *The Sound of Music*, and *Born to Kill*. Clark had sent Wise a stack of scripts he'd written and Wise returned them in person, over coffee, with blunt advice: "You have industry but no talent." Clark knew it was the truth and soon left town.

What were these scripts about? Clark hesitated, though not for as long as a normal liar would have, and he masked the pause with an exasperated look, suggesting that the question was impertinent. The scripts were adaptations, he said, of Ford Madox Ford's *Parade's End*, a quartet of novels about the decline of the British aristocracy after World War One. I told him I found this coincidental, since a BBC-produced version of the novels had aired just that winter on American television. "Oh really?" Clark said. His face turned vague.

"We never talked about film noir," I said, adopting a brisker, more assertive tone meant to put him on notice that I was a free man with places to go and here to clarify certain matters, not to enjoy his ad-libbed reminiscences. "Have you ever thought part of your problem may have been your attraction to such a morbid form?"

"I never liked film noir," he said. "I really don't know where that idea came from."

"Your trial," I said. "It cropped up fairly often."

"I prefer musicals. *Singin' in the Rain*. *It's Always Fair Weather*. That kind of thing."

"Have you ever read Patricia Highsmith's *Ripley* books?"

"Whose? I'm sorry," he stammered. "I've never heard of them."

I'd applied too much pressure; I retreated into small talk, hoping to make him comfortable again. Somehow this led him to offer his thoughts on the "terrible" Boston Marathon bombings, which had occurred the week before. The site of the explosions wasn't far from one of his old haunts, he said, a coffee shop where he and several friends had held a cultural discussion group they called "Cafe Society." Though the bombings did have a bright side, he volunteered. He'd heard that they had displaced his murder conviction as a topic of conversation in Boston.

"I looked up the name of that art dealer you gave me. It opened up quite a mystery."

"Yes?" he said.

He gazed through the partition and seemed to fade, a subtle dissolve into interiority that camouflaged his glee, I sensed, at having snared me yet again. He offered me nothing useful about the art scam, sidestepping or deflecting all my questions and veering off into pat comments on art in general. The topic went flat and the visit got away from me. The next thing I knew he was talking about tea. He told me that his Chichester alias, the one he'd used in San Marino while living on the Sohus property, was a marketing ploy, invented to lend a British feel to a small tea-selling enterprise of his whose customers were "churches and VFW halls." He purchased the tea in bulk and branded it Chichester, representing it as an Old World family firm. Demand for his product was cyclical, he said, and peaked in the months after Christmas, when churches were flush with holiday donations and tended to buy their entire year's tea supply in a single big transaction. This was one more reason, he said, that he couldn't have killed John Sohus in early February 1985: the tea-buying season was in full swing. He was racing all over the state to serve his clients, most of whom were up near San Francisco, hundreds of miles from San Marino.

"Do you have any sales records, maybe? Motel receipts?"

"I slept in my car mostly. It was long ago. The business was very casual," he said. "I also wrote term papers for college students. That was my main thing. They were mostly Iranians."

The phones were muted by whoever controlled them, or maybe they ran on timers. We rolled our eyes and mock-scowled at the receivers, miming our chagrin at being bullied by the jail's peremptory protocols, their emasculating insults and rebuffs. Clark pointed a finger at my chest and then at his, the let's-get-together-again sign. I shrugged while nodding, an intentionally ambiguous combination. Commanded by some figure I couldn't see, he turned and followed a prescribed route out, falling in with the other departing inmates. Back to their drudgery and shamings, their god-awful toilets, their swill, their slit-like windows. At some point he'd said that what held the place together was the big TV inside the dayroom, usually tuned to sports and always mobbed. Clark shunned it. Nor did he participate in the occasional trips up to the roof, which offered a cycloramic view of palm-lined avenues, mountains, freeway systems, down-gliding and ascending jumbo jets. Until his release, he'd rather not see those things. He predicted that day was fast approaching. He was composing a motion for dismissal, giving all his hours to perfecting it; he said it would be irresistibly persuasive, exposing many key witnesses as liars and demonstrating that the legitimate evidence actually proved precisely the opposite of what Balian had claimed it proved. Someone needed to hunt down Linda Sohus, surprise her in her lair, and drag her back here. She wasn't dead, she was out there, lying low. Three months from now, in August, at his sentencing, he'd even tell me she'd been sighted. In the Carolinas, at a stable, working as a horse groomer, possibly under the last name "Schus." It would have been an ingenious alias: "Sohus" with the O switched to a C. A teasing, revealing alias, he said. If spoken aloud or if written with one more last S, it was the German word for "shot."

Clark loved puzzles, everybody knew. Linda loved them too, perhaps, but this one, "Schus," was probably beyond her as a monolingual high-school dropout. Even assuming she wasn't dead—a stretch, since no one besides Clark's "source" had heard a peep from her in decades— she'd obtained quite an education on that horse farm. The more fascinating puzzle, though, was this: why did he bother? And why did he keep bothering? The trial was over, good and over; his life was over too. Fine, he might choose to withhold the truth forever, but why all the anagrams, slipknots, and Kabuki? Why all the shadow-puppet Cheshire cats chasing their own disappearing tails? After my second jailhouse visit in April I pondered these questions on the beach at dusk, walking along the foam-marked tideline kicking a soggy yellow tennis ball that someone had been tossing to a dog. My own lies, and the lies that others told me, were usually fairly simple productions aimed at avoiding or defusing conflict. Few had ever required any rehearsal; I devised them on the spot, often without skill or subtlety, and frequently they were caught immediately or manufactured with so many flaws that I eventually recanted, tired of doing the repairs. The only lies that had ever brought me pleasure, mild pleasure, were those that righted or forestalled some perceived institutional injustice.

But Clark lied to lie, it seemed, like songbirds warble. Or like surfers, serious Malibu surfers, surf, paddling wildly to reach the largest swells so they can hop up and execute their tricks, those long, knifing glides and spray-flinging reversals. So what if they crashed at the end? The ride was worth it. No crash, in fact, no decent ride. Clark, in the arch-wizard years when I first knew him, with his high-earning wife, his sitting, heeling mascots, his pupil-popping private Guggenheim, must have known he was swooshing toward a tumble, must have felt at his back the curling overhang massing to flop and pound him to the bottom. But hang on, hang on, through the shudders and the wobbles—that's the giddy fun of it. Then, crunch. *Kapow.* Then stabilize and get back at it. Prison wasn't the end for him at all. He could still pursue his passion there, machinating in his cell and prevaricating in the mess hall. A tidy setup for a master liar. Over dinner, Ellroy had voiced a theory about the psyches of the damned that struck me as slightly oversteeped in his bitter lemon, cold-water Protestantism. Men like Clark, he said, reached a state of such bewilderment that they unconsciously sought out imprisonment as a way of "radically limiting their choices."

Of all the sleights Clark had ever practiced on me, the one I would have wanted him to sign, had it been a painting or a sketch, occurred at the end of the dinner he didn't pay for in 2002, during my visit to Cornish. After I grumpily gave the waitress my credit card, he'd asked me, as if to distract me from the bill, if I'd like to see a picture of his highly classified propulsion lab. He pulled a color photo from his jacket and laid it on the table beside the pepper shaker. The shot appeared to be taken from a plane and featured a dense, unbroken canopy of green deciduous treetops. I picked it up to get a closer look. All I saw was foliage, no laboratory. I squinted. "It's there. Right there," Clark said. "You're looking at it. It's under all those trees."

SEVENTEEN

PART OF WHAT makes this a California story is that it proves the dime-store mystics right: when you give up pursuing the answers, the answers come, though not the ones you imagined were important, only the ones you never knew to ask for, the ones that ultimately matter, since once you have them you'll never require more. Fifteen years to the week after climbing into my truck to deliver a crippled hunting dog to a man I believed to be a Rockefeller largely because I hoped to be the friend of one, an envelope stuffed with belated revelations arrived at my front door by courier. It came from the Reverend Mary

Piper and her husband, Harry, the brokerage heir, who'd
left Montana a few years earlier and whom I'd last seen in
1998 on the hot July day when I picked up Shelby, their
beloved canine Lazarus. Aided by specialized surgeons, New
Age healers, and the prayers of their church, the Pipers had
virtually raised her from the dead. Mary was a deacon in
those days, about to be ordained a priest, and ministering to
homeless animals was central to her calling. A local Humane
Society official described her once in print as "the Mother
Teresa of Foster Care."

The Pipers had contacted me by phone after reading my
New Yorker story about Clark's trial. They thought I might
be interested in perusing a file on Shelby that they'd assembled in 1998 and saved for all these years, a sort of scrapbook
in her memory. It included printouts of dozens of e-mails
that they'd exchanged with Clark that summer and that
told the story of Shelby's adoption, beginning with Clark's
campaign to win their trust by portraying himself as a caring animal owner. The file also contained a second set of
documents: copies of "The Shelby Report," a collection of
unsigned postings that Clark had written in his distinctive
fabulist style and published on a Web site for Gordon setter
fanciers. The first posting was dated July 19, the day after
I brought Shelby to LaGuardia Airport, and the last one
was dated September 3, when Clark informed his "readers"
(who may have dwindled to the Pipers alone by then, if
indeed there had ever existed any others) that he was suspending the "Report" and hoped that people would keep

him in their prayers. His reasons for this wistful, sudden sign-off were left unstated, but anyone who'd followed the "Report" already knew what they were and was unlikely ever to forget them.

First, I studied the e-mails. Read with illuminated eyes, they told the tale of a predatory snot—a lip-smacking smoothie with arachnid blood. I pictured him perched before his keyboard slurping milky English tea and sniffing the fumes from his drying yellow hair color, nimbly courting and cornering two strangers of pearly faith and optimism. Clark knew how to manipulate the Pipers because he'd presumably read and analyzed "Shelby's Story—Angel in our Midst," Mary's fond account of Shelby's recovery. She'd written it for the Gordon Setter Club's Web site. It had reached Clark's attention, the e-mails indicated, through a friend of his, one Leslie Titmuss, a Maine antiques dealer and private pilot who'd also contacted the Pipers separately about adopting Shelby. Since Leslie had learned of Shelby first, "he should have first pick," Clark wrote, though he wasted no time in denigrating his friend as a reckless boob: "He almost got all of us killed last year flying home from Maine when another jet soared above us a mere 250 feet away on an identical course going the other way. On the same trip he also bounced three times when landing in Caldwell, N.J., and then took off again for another loop." Clark, by contrast, was a prudent fellow, and something of an armchair veterinarian. He flooded the Pipers' inbox with rarefied canine health-food recipes heavy on brewer's yeast and wheat germ, nudging advice on Shelby's

thyroid problems ("You might want to go easy on the medi-
cation . . . Even trying kelp tablets or powder might work"),
and swearing solemn vows of guardianship should the Pipers
entrust him with the dog. He promised, for instance, to keep
her at his side for all but five hours a week, taking her to
work with him at Asterisk LLC, his banking firm, and on his
vacations. For those few hours they couldn't be together, she
would be safe with his "Spanish housekeeper."

The Pipers were charmed. How could they not be
by someone so attuned to canine thinking and behavior
that he could ask, "Does she have the same manipulative
tendencies that Yates has? I mean the excellent begging
skills all Gordons have—deep brown eyes that seem to
say, 'Stilton Cheese . . . Just a little more, please.'" And
how could they not be further charmed by a dog owner
so magnanimous that he let Yates freely lick and slobber
on his peerless modern art collection? In case the Pipers should doubt this, Clark directed them to a lively
piece that had run the year before in *ArtNews*. Its title was
"Spitting Image." His wife had written it. Clark urged
the Pipers to look it up.

The e-mail correspondence, begun in June, had moved
right along; by July Shelby's adoption by Clark was nearly
settled. The Pipers had found in him, or thought they had,
the figure whom they'd been praying for: Shelby's "great
lifetime match." Clark seemed perfect, inconceivably perfect, and thanks to his frisky, detailed letters the Pipers had
a fairly thorough sketch of him: a rich, good-natured, nutri-

tionally scrupulous, naturopathically informed, flexibly scheduled, aesthetically advanced, hilariously daft, happily married Christian gentleman whose other religion was dogs.

But then something troubling occurred. Clark told one rambunctious tale too many, and the Pipers went on alert. The anecdote was set in Houston a few years earlier, when Clark was supposedly running an oil company there and living with Yates in the Four Seasons hotel, which was situated, he said, beside a "Bayou." One blustery day the setter and his master went out for a stroll along this swampy inlet and somehow the animal fell into the water. Clark pulled on the dog's leash—apparently a long one—and hauled him back onto dry land just as a "snake-like thing" swam swiftly toward them. A juvenile alligator.

Clark's account of this close call on the bayou left Mary highly unamused. "Maybe I should have screened you guys more about your extracurricular activities," she wrote in response. "Gotta redo the rescue placement form . . . do you have a vet? Fenced area? Do you allow the dog to chase alligators for fun?" She voiced her concern to the Gordon Setter Club, asking a woman there if she could vouch for Clark. No, in fact, the woman couldn't. Here's why: Clark, under a different name (a privacy measure, he had claimed), had looked at a litter of puppies a few years earlier and said, according to the puppies' owner, "some bizarre things."

The Pipers grew fretful, trading nervous e-mails with the setter folks about whether to pay Clark a "home visit" and inspect him at close range. It was mid-July, and the weeks-long adoption talks had stalled. That's when Leslie Titmuss, the man from Maine, who hadn't written the Pipers for a while, glided back into view. The antiquarian and aviator sent them an e-mail officially confirming his loss of interest in Shelby. He'd fallen for a younger dog, he wrote—an abandoned puppy from Illinois. He did, however, have two friends, he said, under whose roof Shelby was sure to thrive. Mary asked if these people were the Rockefellers. "Yes, they are Clark and Sandy," Titmuss replied. "I couldn't imagine better owners for your dog. They are total dog fanatics." This glowing character reference revived the Pipers' confidence in Clark. It also, apparently, strengthened Mary's religious faith.

"Clark," Mary wrote, no longer wary, "another miracle, God incidence, whatever you name it . . . We had dinner last night with Walter and Maggie Kirn who were planning to escort her on the plane. The evening ended with Walter planning to drive her out this week."

The packet of e-mails, which I'd heavily checkmarked, underlined, and annotated ("Weird," "Shut up!," "Particularly nauseating"), lay spread out on my desk for days. Leslie Titmuss bothered me. His name, it made me want to sneeze. I also thought I recognized it. I typed it into my laptop, a procedure that had lately held far too much suspense for me. Among the top results the search returned was a page from GoodReads, a literary Web site. It was a capsule summary of a novel, *Paradise Postponed,* by the British writer John Mortimer: "Ultraliberal clergyman Simeon Simcox, rector of the village of Rapstone Fanner, leaves his entire fortune to Leslie Titmuss, a social-climbing conservative politician."

I DIDN'T CALL THE Pipers right away, inclined to treat them tenderly after learning how callously Clark had treated them, without their knowledge, in 1998. The bratty literary psychopath hadn't merely toyed with them, he'd mocked them, luring them into a novelistic board game whose rules, objectives, characters, and themes—particularly the rooking of a priest by a ruthless Tory—had been set before they joined the game. They didn't need to reflect upon the fact that the last married couple Clark had fastened on while dreaming of a Titmussian inheritance had suffered the harshest of permanent separations: the husband packed in plastic book bags with tree roots poking through them, and the wife, detectives speculated, dumped off a ledge on the Angeles Crest Highway that sinuously links suburban Los Angeles with the high-desert scrublands around Palmdale.

I'd driven this road a couple of weeks before, on the day of a long-postponed memorial service for John and Linda Sohus put on by their families and friends. It happened that the service was being held in a park just a couple of miles away from the spot where the Angeles Crest begins. I noticed its name on a big sign and made a snap decision to explore it, partly to keep from thinking about the service, which was set to start in half an hour. I knew it would depress me. The Sohuses had died so long ago, and while living

such circumscribed, low-paycheck lives, that very few people would be there to remember them; very few had known
them in the first place. I expected lots of empty chairs. I
expected much leftover snack dip and untouched punch. I'd
find out after my drive that I was right. The only friend of
John I'd see was Colonel Rayermann with his *Star Trek* pin.
He delivered the saddest, most modern eulogy I ever expect
to hear. It centered on all the cool consumer technology
that John, the science nerd and Trekkie, would have loved
but hadn't lived to see. The colonel singled out the flip-up
cell phone. Because it was based on *Star Trek*'s handheld
"Communicator" (a toy version of which was set out on a
table for mourners to gaze upon and handle), John would
have adored it. He also would have adored the iPhone, for
its mighty processing power and small size. The colonel predicted (if that's the word for describing a future that never
was) that John would have invented many amazing apps for
it. This what-if speech had a time-travel effect. Instead of
imagining John living on to use the devices of our day,
I imagined technological progress halting at the moment
of his death in 1985. I imagined John surviving, that is,
and cell phones, laptops, Google, and all the rest of it never
being born. This vision of a barely wired world filled me
with a peaceful feeling, and it seemed very real for a couple
of drifting minutes. Then came the eerie part: in the dusky
woods around the park, a group of coyotes started howling.
Their primordial wails and whines and yips were improba-
bly close by, and louder than the colonel's voice. My inner

sense of historical direction and temporal location simply failed. Maybe coyotes had cell phones before we did. Maybe John was out there on a starship. Maybe Clark was the devil from the Bible. Maybe this was how California feels before plate tectonics break it like a cracker and everyone sighs and says "Finally" and drops straight down into the fissure, their gadgets and wallets spilling from their pockets.

But before I fell into this reverie of slippage I drove the Angeles Crest Highway. I watched from my car for the first low-traffic curve, the first high-altitude turnout near a precipice, where a man in a truck with a body in the bed might feel safe backing up against a gorge and kicking his floppy cargo down the slope, into the stands of spiky yucca plants and ripping, snapping chaparral. Three or four miles farther up the road, the towers of downtown were smoggy columns visible in notches between brown hills, and I started to see beside me on the road evidence of that slothful, piggish streak that rises in people, not only bad ones, when they feel securely unobserved in places that seemingly belong to no one. Burst, spilling bags of diapers lay on the shoulder, empty six-packs, moldering wads of clothing, a busted-up computer monitor whose screen was a few broken fangs of smoky glass. It's in all of us, that quick urge to toss a can, a Styrofoam burger carton, a cigarette butt into the great, no-consequences void. Out of sight, out of mind. But in Clark, I had a hunch, this childish conviction that an unwitnessed action doesn't count operated as a prime directive. Underground to him meant gone. Behind a closed door or a wall meant nonexistent. Two plainly contradictory lies told to two different people were equally authoritative utterances. This thinking dies in most people as children, when mom comes around the corner to see the food we threw, the cat whose tail we wrapped with rubber bands, our brother's toy truck sticking out from under our bed, but in Clark it bred a devious perfectionism. If the trick was correctly planned and deftly executed, the buried horror would never surface, the sealed container would never open, the dupes would never meet to compare notes. The world as he saw it was a concealment mechanism; he didn't carry inside him the constant watchman called conscience or society or God. He lived in two modes, the apparent and the veiled, and in two realms, the opera and the sewer, and he shuttled between them like a genie.

To Frank Girardot, who visited him in jail after I quit paying such calls, he told a story from his Bavarian youth, about creeping out into his village late one night and disassembling several road and traffic signs, which he then attached to different signposts. Village drivers were confused for days, he said. They made wrong turns, set course for the wrong towns, slowed down where they were required to speed up. They couldn't pin down the source of their bewilderment, and finally Clark—then Christian Gerhartsreiter—tired of his neighbors' haplessness and put the signs back where they'd been. I asked Girardot, who'd visited the village while researching a book on Clark (*Name Dropper*, a comprehensive case file on the Sohus murder), if there was any talk of the boy trickster suffering the sort of family abuse that American TV talk shows and trauma memoirs blame for spawning such delinquency. No. Quite the opposite, Girardot said. All his reporting suggested that Christian's parents excused and coddled their naughty son. An angry neighbor would alert them to some mean prank of Christian's and his parents would laugh it off.

IN "THE SHELBY REPORT," the adult Christian ran riot, a rampant fantasist with a masked agenda whose likely motive jumped out at me at the end of my first reading. The posts run from mid-July to early September, from Shelby's arrival in New York to Clark's declaration that he must leave New York and move to some quieter, safer, more remote spot. The early posts are studiously mundane, filled with dramatic re-creations of Shelby's and Yates's morning "hunts" for squirrels in Central Park and supplemented by clinical accounts of their eliminatory behavior. "Low squirrel count—only chased two. Stool normal. She failed to urinate after an hour walk, but did so once we reached the kitchen." Because the posts are intended for the Pipers along with a small, unnamed group of setter lovers, Clark fussily documents Shelby's transformation from wheelchair-bound laggard to prancing purebred. He gives himself all the credit for this upswing; he's the indefatigable Herr Doktor, a peerless fecal analyst. "Stool seems normal, excessive urination finally stopped today. Administered cartilage and thyroid."

The posts hit their stride in early August as Clark contemplates a bracing excursion to Penobscot Bay in Maine. (Perhaps to drop in on Titmuss's antique shop?) Mary Piper writes to register her pleasure. "Really appreciated all the Tron details!!!!!! Thanks!" She drops in some gossip from Montana—the other day, in a town not far from Bozeman, she bumped into a woman who might be one of Clark's cousins, a Rockefeller who uses her married name. Small world! But to Clark, a too-small world. "Gag!" he answers. Then he bashes the woman, hard. Mary is duly chastened, but in offering amends to Clark she unwittingly attracts the wolf. She not only alludes to family money and past depredations upon her vulnerable loved ones, she paints Montana as a game-rich hunting ground as well as a fine place to build a lair: "Sorry to have mentioned it. She does not know that I am aware of her name—she's hiding out here like many people with recognizable names. We are safe here altho if we would have stayed in Mpls. I would have kept my maiden name for sure. Harry's mother was kidnapped and ransomed a number of yrs. ago and no one can forget it and leave him alone."

If Mary hadn't shunned her new acquaintance, the actual Rockefeller dwelling discreetly in Montana, but had quizzed her one day about her New York "cousin," she might have wound up sending bounty hunters to spring from the bushes in Central Park and demand that Clark relinquish Shelby. She might also have kept pressing Clark to cooperate with a newspaper reporter who wanted to name him in a feature article about Shelby's new Cinderella life. Clark promises to consider Mary's request, but suddenly a family scandal intrudes that makes Clark shy about his name. "Horror of Horrors!" he writes, and then reveals the abominable besmirchment: a rogue male member of his noble clan has posed in Jockey boxer shorts for a magazine ad!

As August in Manhattan steams along, the tone of the "Report" grows surly, volatile, and menacingly immature. One senses the sped-up sprouting of a bad seed. Minor, everyday events that feel like pure concoctions nonetheless are crudely molded into goofy fables of confrontation, evasion, and revenge. One bright Tuesday morning in Central Park's Sheep Meadow, an injured squirrel drops from a tree, is temporarily stunned, and then rushes directly at Clark and his two hounds. The rodent's bold frontal maneuver shocks the dogs. Shelby lunges at it and wrecks her wheelchair. The daring squirrel escapes, scrambles back up the tree trunk to its perch, and then, as though to shake its tiny fists at the moping, outfoxed dogs, rains down hard little nuts upon their heads. Such impudence! But the "real-life" fairy tale goes on, because, as every well-bred child knows, there's something that goeth after pride. *Kerplunk!* The squirrel falls off its branch again, the setters bristle, and the squirrel (the king of squirrels?) charges right at them and scores its second triumph. This joust in the park is elusively upsetting. Whether it's based on real events or not, it's Clark's clumsy take on Aesop and A. A. Milne, but with a nasty Three Stooges edge.

In mid-August, only a month since Shelby landed, the "Report" really starts bubbling and fermenting. Sulfurous notes of Edgar Allan Poe can be faintly tasted in the brew. The dogs start fighting for no reason. Shelby catches a bird and, with a "gleeful look," sets its misshapen, mauled body at her master's feet. Then she picks it back up and tortures it some more. Having at last learned to walk without assistance, Shelby now shows no mercy to the lame. Days later, she attacks a "Corgie-mix puppy" that's running free in the park despite a crackdown by "our Nazi mayor," whom Clark refers to in another post as "Adolf," not Rudolph, Giuliani. This mock slip of the tongue is doubly phony because it's also, no doubt, stolen.

August, endless, fetid August. A plague of unknown origins descends upon the House of Rockefeller. For Clark, the first symptoms are a sore throat, sodden lungs, a cough, and mental torpor. Returning one day from his dog walk, he discovers a rash, a spot of redness, on his chest. It seems that in his dazed, thick-headed state he's been wearing his polo shirt inside out—its alligator emblem has rubbed his skin raw. The dogs react to the pathogenic atmosphere with "random agression incidences," including one in which Shelby, now afflicted with chronic diarrhea, leaps on Yates and bites his neck. Soon afterward, Yates fangs Clark's leg. Clark starts neglecting his work. The indebted Third World countries that he has been laboring to keep afloat will just have to paddle harder, or learn to swim.

As Shelby declines, shedding her silky fur in patches,

Clark desperately seeks outside aid. He summons his favorite dog groomer, a "miracle worker" with an exceedingly unconventional name and a unique dual-gender physiognomy. The name is 123, short for the groomer's legal name, which is the groomer's Social Security number. The physical oddity is an extra sex organ that the groomer had surgically attached—that's right, *attached*, not surgically sculpted from flesh already there—to "hir" body. ("Hir" is a hybrid of "his" and "her," Clark says.) The post stopped me cold when I first read it. What the bloody hell? Clark ponders the groomer's pansexual dating life, transfixed by this chimera from his own brain. If this is his way of disclosing to the Pipers, and to setter fanciers everywhere, that he's gay or bi, there are surely easier, less grotesque ways. So why choose this one? I rubbed my chin, but not for all that long. Clark is telling the truth about himself, or at least about how he sees himself. He's a string of digits, not a person. And his penis (really the only sexual organ that can hypothetically be "attached") feels like a piece removed from someone else and sutured onto him.

On August 15, Clark introduces a new and fateful motif, his modern art collection. He wonders if his art is linked somehow to his dogs' declining health, their mucus-coated eyes and bouts of nausea. Most of their vomiting, he notes, occurs in front of his new Motherwell canvas. Might the dogs be allergic to the paint used by the abstract expressionists? His absurd speculation on this point caused me to push back from my desk, convinced that he was pulling something significant, not just gassing and goofing for the fun of it. Besides the Pipers, I don't know who he thought his readers were, but he is setting them up, quite obviously. He wants them to think about his paintings. He wants them to see them in their minds. He even names the particular Motherwell: *Elegy for the Spanish Republic.* Is he advertising the forgery for sale? If it sickens his dogs, he can't keep it, surely. And what about the Hercule Poirot tone? It announces that the "Report" now has a plot, and Clark is going to stick to it.

He sticks to it for the rest of August, converting the "Report" into a kind of medical mystery novel. In the midst of this investigation, he swerves off into an odd, unprompted anecdote whose conspicuous offhandedness feels suspicously premeditated, but to what end? He mentions a stuffed dog toy that Shelby and Yates like to mistreat. He rambles on about the toy. Not coming to a point. Just blathering. The toy has no brain, he comments. (Of course not. So?) His setters, however, do have brains, he says. (Yes? And?) Then, out of nowhere, he comes to the point, the one he seemingly just drifted into. It's a scary point. It's a chilling point. "I guess anyone with brains," he muses, "can easily play rough with someone who has no brains, because if you do not have any brains, you would never know just how hard someone jerks you around."

In August 1998, perusers of "The Shelby Report" had no way of knowing that this casual remark was a doctrinal defense of murder, a sort of philosophical confession, by a criminal practiced in the art—an uncommonly literate criminal who considered murder an art indeed. I can picture Clark typing the post on his computer: his extra-proper schoolboy sitting

posture; his wormy smirk; his bare ankles crossed and rub-
bing. He erases and edits; he fiddles with the syntax, trying to
sound both natural and concise, relaxed and contrapuntal. A
subliminal creepiness is his ideal, like that of a butler decant-
ing ruby port with a badly scratched right hand, an ice cream
truck jingle heard faintly at a funeral, or a black leather glove
in the grass beneath a swing set. He is alone in the house, his
wife out earning, the whole brainless, plodding world out
earning. No one knows who he is or what he's done or what,
like Raskolnikov in *Crime and Punishment* (how many times
he must have studied that book!), he's telling them (without
exactly telling them) about what he's done. The dopes. The
dunces. I picture his dogs beside him as he has these thoughts,
and I think I know why he likes them there: because he's
smarter than they are. Because they're dogs. He can insert his
thoughts into their heads, but they can't put a single thought
in his. Nor can they guess his thoughts. Most people can't,
either, but most people wouldn't be willing to lie here next to
him, reminding him with every breath and whimper, every
involuntary scratching motion, every ignorant doggy thing
they do, that he's the master, he's Merlin, he's Mr. Ripley.
Outside the house, among people, he proves it constantly, but
he likes to feel it inside the house as well.

As he sits at his desk and writes about his dogs, he's really
writing about other things. He's transforming abominable,
secret episodes into cute stories that he can tell at dinner.
He's figuring out ways to tell the truth so that it will sound
made up, like bombast, like blarney, like more of Clark's

BS. He's also making up stuff that will sound true, at least to people without brains—people like me back in 1998. Did I have a brain back then? I believed I did. I believed it was quite a developed brain, in fact. It had studied at Princeton and Oxford and written novels. It had jigsawed together raw copy from far-flung stringers to fashion respectable cover stories for *Time*. So why did it fail me? For the last time, why?

"The Shelby Report," as I reached the last few posts, was leading me toward a "Eureka!" I could feel it. It was creeping up like a head cold, like a fever. It was going to be one of those Perry Mason moments that seasoned trial reporters joke about, insisting that they never happen. At Clark's trial (and at most such trials, I'll bet, where murder still has an element of mystery), I'd hear someone say every day, or couple of days, "This isn't Perry Mason." It meant that certain dramatic turns weren't coming. It meant that we were in Los Angeles, not Hollywood. It meant that a star witness for the prosecution, though his eyes were darting around the room, wasn't going to be trapped by the defense and admit that he and Clark had once been lovers, and Clark had left him, and his testimony was all a lie dreamed up to take revenge. It meant most of all that the heavyset old lady sitting quietly in the back row, who people assumed was at the trial because her TV or her air conditioner was broken, was not going to yank off her long gray wig and startle us all with her true identity: Linda Sohus, alive, the Unicorn Killer!

It didn't matter what others thought; I knew such unmaskings and turnabouts were possible. I'd experienced a few already. I'd had a friend once, see, a rich eccentric. I brought him a crippled dog one summer. He showed me his Rothkos. He took me to his club. Years went by. I visited his mansion. I held his hand through his divorce. Then I turned on the news one day, and there he was. No one I knew.

But now I knew him better.

Late August 1998. "The Shelby Report" is building toward a climax. Why is the poor setter still declining? Why can she hardly breathe in the apartment? "I just cannot think of what might bother her," Clark writes. "If anyone has any clue on how to solve this mystery, let me know." By then, of course, Clark's readers know the answer and are waiting for him to catch up: the paintings are somehow posioning the dogs. And sure enough, after a quick trip up to Maine, where the dogs' symptoms promptly disappear, Clark uncovers the secret. The allergen is linseed oil, the base of the paint in every work he owns!

This is terrible news, Clark tells his readers (though only the Pipers have any reason to care, having put their darling Shelby in his hands), because most of the paintings are so large that they simply can't be moved, not even from room to room. There is only one solution, he concludes: he and Shelby must go away at once—far, far away, not just out of the apartment. They have to leave the city! This seems awfully rash, a gross overreaction to an abstract expressionism allergy, which is probably why Clark piles on the horror to justify his flight from the metropolis. Two dismal events occur on the same day. As Clark watches helpless and aghast, a Parks Department truck runs down a dog in cold blood. "ON PURPOSE," he writes. Then, after that—or perhaps before that; the post is confusing on this point—a random miscreant pulls a knife on him. New York has become a "hellhole," he laments. Worse, Shelby's life is still endangered. (Clark makes her sniff linseed oil to test his theory, and, alas, it pans out, confirmed by the scientific method.) What will happen next to man and dog? Where in the world will they go after New York?

Clark leaves things there. On September 3, 1998, he bids farewell to his readers and declares that "The Shelby Report" is going dark after a run of not even two months. "Please keep us in your prayers," he writes.

And then, on September 8, just five days later, he sends a personal e-mail to the Pipers, Harry and Mary, the Reverend and the heir. They included it in the file they sent me, clipped to the very bottom of the stack, right where it would have been found on *Perry Mason*. In it, Clark tells them that he fears he's approaching a nervous breakdown. He has been playing them all summer, of course, assiduously, patiently, and obliquely, first with the help of the fictional Leslie Titmuss, and then with the aid—or through the use—of their angelic Shelby. He has also been calling me during this time, though oddly he has never breathed a word to me about "The Shelby Report," in which I would have been interested, presumably, considering that I'm the pliant oddball who drove and flew the dog across America. I did it, in part, as a favor to the Pipers, who contacted me as a favor to him, Clark. And now, in the fall of 1998, he is writing them for another favor. Not a favor from them, it seems, but from me—the person the Pipers persuaded to help him last time and the only person who can supply him with what he now tells them he desperately needs.

The e-mail is very specific about his needs. He needs a place in Montana. A place to live. A quiet place to write his *Star Trek* books. A place to complete his "Constance Garnett rewrites." The Pipers, who never caught on to Leslie Titmuss, may not be familiar with Constance Garnett, either, but I write novels and I sure am. She translated the Russian masters, including Dostoyevsky. Meaning, if I read Clark's thoughts correctly, he's planning a little touch-up of *Crime and Punishment* in September 1998. Perhaps he'll personaliize it in some way. Once he finds a place to live and work, that is. He asks the Pipers to be on the lookout for a "a small furnished garage apartment on a working ranch that allows dogs . . . The less the better, probably. Just a small room would do fine."

I had such a place in 1998—exactly such a place. And Clark, from speaking to me, knew I did. The Pipers might not have known, however, having never come to visit my dog-filled working ranch with a garage. This may be one reason they never thought to tell me about Clark's little wish list. I might not have gotten back to them in any case. I was busy revising my oft-rejected novel and preparing for the baby. I spent that fall on the ranch, holed up, cocooned, doing what a writer and husband should: working, worrying, providing. Later on, in the winter, Clark did mention a visit to my place (in passing, and not a long visit, I gathered) but

I was weeks away from fatherhood, so I told him no. If the Pipers—sweet people whom I truly admired—had spoken to me on his behalf, I might have softened. I might have let Clark come for a short stay, two weeks or maybe three, while he hunted for another place. But he wouldn't have hunted, and I might not have made him, and Maggie—an animal rescuer like Mary—would have melted for Shelby, I just know. How would I have handled that situation? I might have sold Clark a corner of my ranch; I was thinking of parting with a few acres anyway. Money was tight and my obligations were mounting and five hundred acres, if it's divided right, can allow for a neighbor you never have to see, a house or a cabin you never have to look at. Clark might still be living there, if this had happened; Montana, as the Pipers correctly told him, is a very good hideout. And he needed one.

I might not still be there with him, though. I might not be anywhere at all. Clark, who'd always longed to be a writer but lacked some essential literary serum that dwells not in the brain but in the blood, might have been seeking another metamorphosis. If a few well-aimed blows to John Sohus's skull could bring him mastery of *Star Trek*; if walloping Dickie Greenleaf with an oar could turn Tom Ripley into a man of leisure; if driving a chisel into a schoolboy's head could raise Leopold and Loeb to *Übermenschen*; then maybe Clark could find some way, some night, after toiling all day in my garage to translate *Crime and Punishment*, to turn himself, at a stroke, into a writer. He knew a perfect victim when he saw one, and I'd sacrificed myself for him before.

EIGHTEEN

AROUND THE COURTROOM, which was like a movie set, regimented and casual by turns, either all business or all small talk, a popular topic of idle conversation was whether Clark had committed other murders. There was no evidence that he had, but everyone these days is an amateur criminologist, filled with TV-based knowledge that only the experts had once, about supposedly different types of killers. The common killer, Americans have learned, is an impulsive narcissist who, when intoxicated or under stress, ruptures emotionally and lashes out. The serial killer is bereft of empathy and tends to develop in well-known stages, first setting fires and harming animals and eventually graduating to murder, which makes him feel powerful and in control. Was Clark a serial killer, people wondered? He certainly had the look and feel of one. If so, though, why had he retired so early, after claiming just one or two victims? This wasn't standard. It didn't fit the model.

After the trial, when I finally learned about his search for a guest place on a ranch, he seemed to fit the model better. His lust for "rough play" with people he perceived to have no brains hadn't left him, it appeared, but arranging and getting to the games was a tricky, daunting problem for someone who didn't legally exist and had long been ducking the authorities. He couldn't open a bank account or present ID to airlines. He couldn't even risk a traffic violation. When he fled with Snooks to Baltimore, his plan, I'm convinced, was to meet a boat or ship—dispatched, perhaps, by his friend in Peru, who apparently had started a shipping company since leaving the art world—and depart from the United States by sea. The leaky old catamaran he'd bought would be found in the ocean, probably, sinking and adrift, making it seem that he and Snooks had drowned. The manhunt would be over.

But then, while at my desk one night reading the documents the Pipers had sent me, I grew convinced that Clark had murdered again—and that I'd known his victim personally. He chose her well. She was trusting, easily manipulated, and his inferior, socially and mentally, which Clark knew by his old test: she considered him a friend.

"The Shelby Report" was my first clue. Clark's professed romance with his dogs seemed histrionic, as bogus as the rest of him, and the way he exploited the dogs' alleged breakdowns and spasms of viciousness for moldy pathos, shoddy laughs, and sighing admiration (how adorable that he let them lick his art, and how princely that he owned so much of it that he could remain sanguine when they puked on it) felt icily theatrical. How he'd whipsawed the poor Pipers with all his melodramatic crap.

"Mary," I said, when I finally shared with her my conclusions about Clark's treatment of her and Harry, "I looked up Leslie Titmuss, from the e-mails." As soon as I said this, I wished I hadn't called; I saw the shadow of my motives. I was trying to show off to her, bragging about my cryptographic acumen. But I'd already done it, so I did the rest. "Titmuss is from a novel. He was a trick."

"I'm not surprised," she said. She did sound disappointed, though. Perhaps that's how it was to be a priest: you remained ever hopeful even about the worst of us, and bad news about the soul of any one of us struck you as bad news about us all.

Mary then repeated the story I'd heard from Clark: Shelby was run over by a car. I asked her why she believed this to be true and she told me about a visit to Clark's Cornish house in November or December 2000. Her description of the weekend reminded me of my time there, the same cold bedroom, the same paucity of food, except that the Pipers had gotten much closer than I had to meeting J. D. Salinger. They went to his house, or a house Clark said was his. Clark knocked on his door while they hung back. No one answered, Mary said. She remembered the weekend as creepy and uncomfortable except for the pleasure of seeing Shelby again. She seemed healthy, and was walking without her wheelchair. They watched her run and play on Clark's broad lawn.

A week or two later the phone call came. Shelby had been struck down on the road. Clark sounded distraught. "I'm devastated. Just devastated," he said.

"This might seem odd, but I have to ask," I said to Mary. "Did Clark ask for anything? Before you left? Any kind of favor?"

Mary didn't think so. Then something clicked. Well, yes, as it happened, Clark had asked for Harry's help. He wanted Harry to write a letter to the membership committee of the Lotos Club in support of his application to join.

"What was weird," Mary said, "is that Harry's not in that club. I think Clark overestimated his influence."

"But Harry agreed to write the letter?"

"He did," she said.

"And then, not all that long after he agreed, Clark called and told you Shelby was dead?"

"If you're saying what I think you're saying, I don't think I can do this now," said Mary. Whether what she thought I was saying was probable, possible, unknowable, ridiculous, or wicked of me even to suggest, I couldn't quite tell, and I didn't plan to ask.

———

THE LAST TIME I saw Clark was in Judge Lomeli's empty courtroom, with no one to watch us but Lincoln and Washington. During the trial I'd used their portraits as targets for the focal readjustments that I practiced to ward off headaches. Lincoln sat, one fist propped under his chin. He was the thinker, inclined to skepticism. Washington stood moon-faced and broad-chested as though atop a captured hill. He was the hero, prone to secret backaches. The American flag in the corner hung straight down, wilted and exhausted. Clark had been sentenced to life without parole that day. He'd represented himself, and done it poorly. He opened by asking to read a motion he'd written, a ragged sheaf of pages that he carried into court the way that fleeing bank robbers do, in movies only, I'm certain, hugging slipping wads of loot against their bodies. The judge refused his request to hold us spellbound, and Clark looked even more mortified than when he'd heard the verdict read. To spite us all, he withdrew the unheard motion, which I saw was written in pencil. The judge said reporters who wished to interview Clark could do so privately, and take their turns.

"I don't trust you. You betrayed me," he said, when I sat down with him at the defense table, a couple of hours later, after the bailiff had cleared the room and the reporters in line ahead of me had finished up and gone away. Clark had heard that I was writing about him; I'd never mentioned it to him myself.

"I don't trust you either," I said to Clark once he tired of scolding me. It was the perfect, only retort, of course.

His face looked rubbed away somehow, tired and indistinct, like a document that had been photocopied a few too many times. Only around his mouth did some liveliness remain.

"Listen, I'm sorry you feel betrayed," I said, "but I'm writing about you because that's what I do. I'm a writer. You always knew that. And you're a fascinating human being."

"I absolutely am not," he said. Not human? For a moment, that's what it had sounded like to me. It would have been a good joke, though an unlikely one from a stranger to self-deprecating irony. He couldn't discern it when others used it, either; I'd noticed that about him early on, whenever I poked fun at myself with some light story of a screw-up or minor failure. He'd just stare and wait for me to finish. There were blanks in him.

"What happened to Shelby, anyway?" I said. "I know she died, but what exactly happened?" I feigned a forgetful, absent manner, as though I'd recently started growing old.

"She was hit by a car," he said. "Run over."

"When?"

"2000, 2001. Somewhere in there. I can tell you who did it. His name is Peter Burling, a senator. A state senator, not federal. You can ask him. He hit her. Peter Burling."

He strained at the handcuffs that locked him to his chair. It was his way of saying he'd write the name down for me if only all this—the trial, jail, Los Angeles, society, morality, rotten luck, crews of laborers digging in the earth, the durability of bone, stupid people, humiliated Germany, black-and-white movies, suspenseful books, voyages beyond the stars, Jehovah, a man with a mustache, ex-wives and girlfriends, and steel—weren't stopping him from moving his silly arms.

THREE OR FOUR DAYS later I called Peter Burling at his home in Cornish. He said he'd read my piece about the trial, liked it, and was glad to help me. He told me the whole story. He began by acknowledging that he disliked Clark intensely, and he explained why. When Clark moved to Cornish in 1999, Burling was influential in the village, a prominent local leader, and Clark, he said, seemed resentful of him, jealous. For example, Burling had owned a local church—an old and historic Episcopal chapel—and when he tried to grant it to the town, Clark paid the town to turn it over to him. In another strong-arm move, he sought to have the public road that ran beside his house condemned so he could use it as private driveway. Burling said Clark was so intent on hurting him that he once tried to bribe a housekeeper to rifle through his personal files. Burling also believed Clark was a burglar who would enter neighbors' unlocked homes on the pretext of delivering gifts of wild honey. A selfish, secretive, malicious fellow. That Clark had accused him of running down his dog didn't surprise him, Burling said. The truth was, no one had run it over. He knew this because a neighbor woman and he had been the ones to find the body, he said. Shelby was lying peacefully on her side at precisely the spot where Clark's driveway

joined the road. No blood. No wrenched limbs. No ruf-
fled fur. "No indicia of trauma of any kind. I thought that
maybe it had a heart attack."

"Could she have been poisoned?"

"Possibly," Burling said. "All I know is that she wasn't
run over. It looked like she had just laid down to sleep."

Burling excused himself for an appointment and we said
goodbye. I sat and thought for a while at my desk. Shelby
lay on the spot where Clark's driveway joined the road. The
road he wanted condemned? The road that he felt compro-
mised his privacy? The road the town refused to let him
have, and which he then blamed for killing his precious setter? I e-mailed Burling to ask if this road feud was running
hot at the time of Shelby's death. His response was prompt
and slightly formal.

"Platt Road," read his e-mail, "is where the dog's body
was, and the talk about closing the road was contemporane-
ous with the poor dog's death."

Clark had put the setter to good use. Portraying himself as
the savior of her health had helped him secure a letter from
Harry Piper commending him to the Lotos Club. And by
killing her promptly after that was handled, as I was almost
certain he'd done, he'd bolstered his case for closing a public
road that bothered him and which he thought should be his.

Though maybe he had another motive. Or ten of them.
Because Clark had no shortage of motives for murder. To
take. To diminish. To win. To mock. To silence. To supplant.
To not be bored. To create another absence so as not to be

left with your own. Infinite motives, but just one super-motive: to gain an advantage or lose a disadvantage. This was also the motive for lying, the very same, although lying was quicker, cleaner, and much less strenuous. No chopping, no sawing, no shoveling, no mopping. Clark must have loathed such demeaning physical drudgery, and there was no evidence that he'd ever stooped to it—other than those one or two times. Lies, those little murders, were more his style. Big murders, he'd learned the hard way, were perhaps more trouble than they were worth.

He was an artful liar, it was true, and he had tried to be an artful murderer, but he wasn't a real artist, and he knew it. He wasn't even a real artiste, just a simulated man of taste. He wasn't a real forger, just a collector of forgeries. He wasn't a translator of anything, just a would-be "corrector" of others' translations—from languages he didn't know. So what was he? That was his whole predicament: he worked in a form that didn't exist.

Back in fictional 1985 (meaning 2013, when Clark invented the "memory") during his fabled meeting with the great director Robert Wise, Clark self-diagnosed himself about as well as a human being can. "You have industry, but no talent," Wise supposedly told him. I'm confident that Clark believed it, that it represents his true self-image.

After his sentencing, he told me he'd always wanted to write, and he had written, in fact—dog stories on computers, a novel of stupefying length, in pencil—but he'd never had an audience. I suppose that this left him only dupes and victims, a kind of captive audience unaware of its role or its captivity. And dogs, of course, who are similar. And me. I was part of his audience, he thought. But in truth I was acting much of the time. He was conning me, but I was also conning him. The liar and murderer and heaven knows what else was correct about the writer: I betrayed him.

In the empty courtroom after his sentencing, the last time in this life that I would sit with my old friend, and just a few minutes before a guard walked over to unlock him from his chair and guide him by the elbow through a door, I asked him about his other dog, Yates. I was running low on questions by then, and I'd already run out of interest. Liars are exhausting people. Conversing with him was aging me, depleting me. All my questions drew the same response from him, just phrased in different ways. His evil was his prodigious, devouring appetite for other people's vitality and time, which he consumed with words, words, words, word, words. Clark loved to talk but had nothing much to say, nothing of his own, which was surely another reason that he lied, and plagiarized lies, and recycled his old lies. He had ten thousand ways to tell you nothing. I felt like I'd heard all of them.

"Whatever happened to Yates?" I asked.

"Oh, same idea," Clark said, because it was always the same idea with him. "He was old anyway. But he was also run over. It was very sad."

ACKNOWLEDGMENTS

With thanks to Robert Weil, Eric Simonoff, Henry Finder, Frank Girardot, James Ellroy, Will Dana, Frank Foer, Michael Lustig, Curtis Cooke, William Menaker, and CBS News. You tried to keep me on track and mostly succeeded. With special gratitude to Harry and Mary Piper for making themselves vulnerable to me after being so horribly fooled by him. And with loving appreciation for Maisie and Charlie Kirn, who didn't ask to be the children of a writer but do a wonderful job anyway.

ABOUT THE AUTHOR

Walter Kirn is the author of *Thumbsucker* and *Up in the Air*, both made into major films. His work has appeared in the *New York Times*, *The New Yorker*, *The Atlantic Monthly*, *Vanity Fair*, *GQ*, *Esquire*, and *Rolling Stone*. He is the national correspondent for the *New Republic*. He lives in Livingston, Montana.